This story is based on real people and events. For the sake of individual privacy, most names have been changed.

A special thanks to Mark Johnson for his help in crafting this work and a very special thanks to Vandana Singh for all of her love and support.

I would like to thank the reader for going on this journey with me. The subject matter spoken of within these pages can be complex and deserves perfection in articulation.

I apologize to the reader if you find that I do not possess the skill and eloquence of such authors as Ayn Rand, Thomas Sowell, or Alexander Dumas.

I would prefer to tell you my story in person rather than trying my hand at authoring a book. However, my belief in the necessity for people to hear my story, and the impracticality of meeting everyone in person has led to the publication of this book. Please enjoy.

Contents

Before We Get Started

It was midday, late in the summer of 2003, on one of those pristinely sunny days in Portland, Oregon, when the sky is so clear that you can see the majestic Mt. Hood off in the distance. I was out walking in the affluent, predominantly white neighborhood that had been my home for the past three years while I attended the law school located about a mile away. That afternoon, I was enjoying the weather and studying flash cards for the upcoming Oregon State Bar exam.

I was minding my own business when, all of a sudden, two police cars pulled up alongside me and stopped. Normally, it would be unusual to see any police cars in the neighborhood. But suddenly I was looking like a deer in the headlights as I stared down two police cars. The doors opened and four police officers—two to a car, all white—emerged. The driver of the first car waved for me to come closer.

"What are you doing?" one of the officers barked. It felt more like an accusation than a question. A little taken aback by the officer's tone, I responded calmly despite feeling offended. "I'm using these flashcards to study for the Oregon Bar Exam," I said. "Why do you ask?" With his tone unchanged, he went on: "We got a report of a suspicious person walking in the neighborhood." There was a long and awkward silence.

With a hint of sarcasm, I offered, "I have not seen any suspicious-looking people walking in the neighborhood. In fact, I've been walking for about an hour, and besides myself, I haven't seen anyone else walking."

Deprived of an opportunity to continue accosting me, he could only give a flustered response of "ok, well...stay on the sidewalk" before motioning for the other officers to get back in their cars and drive away.

I never found out who called the police. I never had a chance to meet and talk with them about how, with just a glance, their perceptions had already been formed and acted upon to my detriment. I never had the opportunity to tell them that I had grown up in Detroit and lived in both its worst projects and one of its best neighborhoods, nor that I had graduated from a Catholic high school, nor that I had obtained a bachelor's degree. They did not give me the time to share that I spent nearly six years in Japan and that, at one time in my life, I considered myself completely fluent in spoken Japanese. To top it all off, I had just obtained a Juris Doctorate from a well-respected law school nearby, and on the afternoon they made that snap judgment, I was not causing trouble in the neighborhood; I was preparing for the Oregon State Bar. On that afternoon, none of that mattered to whomever placed that call to the police. Unbeknownst to me, the mere color of my skin had communicated to the caller that I was a threat, a bogeyman or possibly a hardened criminal.

You never get comfortable being viewed suspiciously just "for being." That afternoon, my country was one hundred and thirty-plus years removed from slavery, but as the police drove away, I felt as though I had just been ordered to show my freedom papers.

A few minutes after the police left me alone and in one piece, a blonde classmate of mine named Sara drove up alongside me smiling from ear

4

to ear. "Hey, you headed to school? Would you like a ride in my new birthday present?" I said yes and accepted her kind offer. As we rode, I congratulated her on her new ride and with a small degree of envy mentioned that I was going to law school so that I could get a Range Rover, and her parents got her a Range Rover so that she could go to law school. We both chuckled and to keep the atmosphere light, I decided not to mention my encounter with Portland's finest.

Once on campus, we separated, and my mind raced in the direction of constitutional law in search of enough elements for a lawsuit. I could no longer concentrate on my tax law flashcards. Instead, I focused on trying to present my case to the imaginary court in my head and the bitter irony of what just happened as it pertained to a particular day in a class I just completed.

The class was called "The Philosophy of Jurisprudence" and the topic that day was the pros and cons of Affirmative Action policies. The professor was a middle-aged white man known for his liberal politics, and it was clear that he was sincerely in favor of Affirmative Action policies. He explained that Affirmative Action is a great idea because it gives African Americans an opportunity to better themselves, become successful, leave the ghetto, and live in his neighborhood, which he explained was predominantly white and affluent. It was basically like the neighborhood where I lived and was accosted by the cops for the infraction of "walking-while-black."

What my professor said sounded right at face value, but it just didn't feel right to me. My professor was a great guy. He meant no harm and believed in what he was saying. In fact, I could have been considered a textbook example of a black guy that was accomplishing what Affirmative Action policies had intended. I was successful in the sense that I had escaped the ghetto and was living in an affluent white neighborhood.

However, I couldn't consider residing in an affluent neighborhood to be a real prize if the vast majority of my neighbors were white and I was always a suspect. As I sat there listening to my professor go on about this, I just couldn't help myself. I spoke up with "Why should I have to strive to live in your neighborhood?" I challenged. "Why do I have to separate myself from black people to be considered successful?"

My professor and my classmates, all of whom were white, looked at me as if I were speaking Japanese. I got the sense that, like myself, no one else had ever seriously addressed that question. As what I said lingered in the air, they sank in their seats in fearful anticipation of my metamorphosis into the Incredible Black Hulk or the Angry Black Man. "I know none of you mean any offense," I added.

The professor tried, but he could not adequately answer my question. I moved on from law school, but over the years the question continued to linger in my mind. I have come to realize that it was not a question that my professor needed to answer in the first place. It was a question that other Afro-Americans and I should answer ourselves.

This book is my attempt at an answer. As I take you on this journey, I will introduce people and experiences to you. Please keep in mind that my intent is not to berate, belittle, or condemn the individuals or places mentioned *within these pages. I intend to try and provide a different perspective on things and start a critical conversation.*

Part I

Chapter 1

A Paradise Called the Brewster Projects

One night, while my mom and I sat eating our TV dinners and laughing at something so funny on our small black-and-white television that we were both in tears, we were suddenly interrupted by a commotion.

A series of loud, urgent bangs hammered our back door. It opened to a corridor connecting our upstairs unit to three other units in Detroit's Brewster Projects. None of our neighbors would ever step foot in that corridor, unless it were a dire emergency, because junkies would break in and get high there and homeless people would often sleep there, too. It was always dark and creepy, even during the day. The lights never worked, and it smelled like piss. It was a place where bad things happened, so it was the ultimate trump card, for me and my friends, in any game of dare.

But that night, the door that had never been knocked on before was now being tested for its integrity. Over the thunderous vibrations that flooded us with a tidal wave of anxiety, my mother yelled, "Who is it?" And I could feel the surprise and concern in her voice.

The answer came back swiftly: *BOOM BOOM BOOM*!

For the first time, it seemed as if something bad was about to happen to me through no fault of my own.

"Who is it?" she called again.

BOOM BOOM BOOM!

Fear flashed over my Mother's face and she was shaking all over.

"I don't have any money for you to take!"

"We know."

It was an eerily calm response.

A few seconds passed—just long enough to fuel our hope that whomever was on the other side of the door had been deterred. But then, with renewed intensity, we heard it again: *BOOM BOOM BOOM!* Heavy and determined shoulders pummeled against the door. The two dead bolts were hanging on for *our* dear lives. It seemed as if the entire wall would come down along with the door at any moment.

This was not a neighbor's emergency. This was *our emergency.*

"I'm calling the police!" My mother yelled out, finally.

This was my first experience confronting immediate danger and I was overwhelmed with a horrible feeling of complete helplessness. My mother, my guardian and shield from all things bad, wore a look of dread on her face that I had never seen before and will never forget.

Up until that evening, my childhood had been simple, worry-free, and full of love and adventure. I was just a nappy-headed seven-year-old whose face usually carried a smile from ear to ear. But the panic from the back door and in my mother's eyes did not allow my face the luxury of its usual grin.

That night took place during the Cool Era of the 1970s. Brotherly love was in the air, and music seemed to be the very oxygen of the Brewster Projects. Residents would sing on the street corners, and competitions among

9

the more talented populace would sometimes spontaneously combust for the entertainment of pedestrians.

The music of choice was rhythm-and-blues or gospel. Whether walking or driving, people were floating down the street on the smooth sounds of Marvin Gaye, Smokey Robinson, and Diana Ross. Bands like the Isley Brothers and the Spinners kept the Brewster Projects constantly grooving.

To go along with the smooth music about love, politics, and God was the colorful attire people wore: bell-bottom pants, platform shoes, shirt collars wide enough to give the impression that a person could take flight with a strong gust of wind. A nicely picked and evenly trimmed afro was the hairdo du jour. Everyone I encountered seemed pleasant and content. The demeanor was just ... cool. So much so that people even smoked "Kool" cigarettes, its name a perfect complement to their demeanors. The project characters spoke in a smooth, laid-back cadence.

"You know what I'm saying, Youngblood?"

"Yeah, man. I can dig it."

Back then I was often addressed by older males who didn't know my name as Little-brother, Blood, Youngblood, Young-buck, Cool-breeze, or Shorty. Older women who didn't know me would call me Sugar or Honey, just as members of my own family did. People just had a way of addressing one another that was somehow informal yet dignified at the same time. It made everyone seem like family. Everything seemed to be taken care of. There was no hurry or intensity.

People around me identified with being cool. Even one of Detroit's most notorious gangs at the time had a cool name that they borrowed from a late Hollywood film star: the Errol Flynns. There was even a dance called the Errol Flynn.

I loved the Brewsters. It had everything a child could want. Everyone cooked great soul food; you just had to walk around outside to experience the delicious aromas of everything: fried chicken, fried fish, smothered pork chops, collard greens, macaroni-and-cheese, and peach cobblers, on any given day of the week. Occasionally, I'd catch a whiff of someone preparing chitterlings. The particular aroma of pig intestines being cleaned made me vow never to eat them.

The Brewsters were a sprawling reddish-orange maze several city blocks long and several city blocks wide. It was crowded and lively. The only variations from the two-story flats like the one I lived in were two very tall towers and a massive recreation center. It had basketball courts, and some of the greatest players around would compete daily just for a chance to play. Stop by the Brewster Projects, and it is easy to see why blacks from poor neighborhoods dominate the NBA. Often, there may only be one decent basketball court in the whole neighborhood. Competition in the basketball skills market would naturally weed out those who could not play well.

There were also plenty of interesting diversions in the neighborhood for small kids; there were several playgrounds, and the penny candy store was a twenty-minute walk away from my front door. Every day seemed to be filled with some form of excitement. Occasionally, my friends and I would watch the cops catching criminals and sometimes even spot Detroit's S.W.A.T. team arranging themselves in strategic positions, ready to pounce.

There were dogfights and alleyway gamblers. Peek behind certain buildings, and you'd find various forms of shady adult activities hidden away from law enforcement officers but in plain sight of curious kids. A lot of things that were going on in the projects were unseemly, if not outright illegal, but I did not consider this environment dangerous. It was incredibly exciting to a seven-year-old. It was all I knew. My ignorance was my bliss.

My world consisted of my mother and father, my aunt and uncle, and extended maternal family members. Except for my father, who I saw every weekend, we all lived in the projects. Besides visits to my father's apartment, I rarely left the physical boundaries of the Brewster projects back then, and I never left the metaphysical limits of the black culture I was being raised in.

Just a few hours before the banging on the door, I had finally been able to achieve two of my life's goals. The first was learning how to whistle, and the second was learning how to blow a bubble with bubble gum. That day, I'd proudly demonstrated my new skills to my mother. At first, it was to her amusement—but eventually, it just annoyed her.

My sensei for those two lessons was my neighbor, Michelle. Although I had a lot of friends, Michelle and a youngblood named Enith were by far my best friends. Enith, like me, was a typical black kid living in the Brewsters. However, in addition to being a girl, Michelle, her father, mother, and older brother were a complete anomaly—a rare white family who lived in the Brewsters.

12

It didn't seem to make any difference in how Michelle was treated. Older ladies in the neighborhood would call her Sugar or Honey just the same. Through my seven-year-old eyes, apart from the obvious difference in skin complexion, I perceived only a few differences between us boys and Michelle. Physically, she was taller, stronger, and it seemed peculiar that she could not grow an afro.

Michelle's hair flowed down her head and would blow in the wind. My afro would stand firmly at attention even in a storm. She seemed to have fun whenever her mother would comb her hair, and her mother seemed to get just as much pleasure from combing it. Meanwhile, my hair was so coarse that even the thought of having it combed brought shivers down my spine, so much so that I avoided the ordeal to the point of getting threatened with a belt. That's why I so enthusiastically welcomed my older cousin's offers to braid my hair in cornrows, which spared me from the trauma of having my hair combed for days, or even weeks, if the cornrows were maintained well.

Besides a few typical childhood bumps and bruises, nothing bad ever happened to me in the Brewsters until that spring night in 1978, with our back door being beaten like a drum. Something ominous was beckoning. Things were going to change.

Boom Boom Boom!

My mother and I could hear them mumbling on the other side of the back door. There were clearly at least two men. Despite the fear in her heart and the tremble in her hands, she kept her voice calm when she spoke to the 911 operator.

13

"Hello," she said, to the operator, her tone even and deliberate as if she were ordering a pizza. "There are two men at my back door trying to break in. We're at 692 Mack Avenue in the Brewster projects."

But when the person on the other end asked a question, my mother's calm broke, "Yes," she replied, practically screaming. "They are trying to break in now! They know I'm alone here with my son!"

The phone was hanging on the wall in the kitchen, and whomever was on the other side of the door could hear my mother's conversation.

Boom Boom Boom!

Then, finally, one of the bangers shouted, "We'll be back!"

Just as fast as it started, the assault on our back door ceased, and the evil men were gone, and with them our sense of security. Within minutes of the last bang on our back door, five police officers, a few relatives, and a few of our neighbors crowded into our small apartment. The police had arrived almost instantly. They were white men with varying expressions of concern, annoyance, and weariness on their faces. In contrast, the neighbors all reminded me of the elders in our church, praising God that we were okay. They showed great concern for our safety, denouncing yet another act of evil by lowlife hoodlums.

Soon enough, my mother and the neighbors were throwing names of potential suspects at the police. Though I had no idea of who Mark and Jessie were, they became the prime suspects by consensus. Soon after that, the police started to leave our apartment, and as they walked out, each one made sure to tell me not to be afraid, and that everything was going to be okay. I believed

14

them. Eventually, I got into my bed, and somehow, despite the evening's events, I fell fast asleep.

The next morning, my mom and I went about our normal routine. She got me ready for school and sent me off with Michelle and Enith before she headed off downtown to the bank where she worked as a teller. On the way to school, I told Michelle and Enith all about what happened the night before. Michelle asked if I was scared. Both of them were already snickering before I answered.

I confidently let the lie roll off my tongue. "No, I wasn't scared."

They burst into laughter and called my bluff.

"Okay," I admitted. "I thought I was going to piss my pants."

Unlike the night before, it was an uneventful school day. Even though the events of the night before stayed with me, their potency was rapidly fading. By the time I was heading home for the day, I was laughing and joking around with my friends as usual.

As we got near our apartments, I could see a moving van near my front door. We all had the same question on the tips of our tongues: Who is moving out now?

People were constantly moving into and out of the Brewsters. One day it could be an elderly resident who died; the next, it would be someone being dragged out by the cops. Cop cruisers, ambulances, and moving vans were a common sight in the Brewsters. But unlike the first two vehicles, the moving van was not always a sign of bad news. It was more often a harbinger of better things to come.

The celebratory moving van would be accompanied by adults slapping one another's backs and shouting praises to the Lord. They'd say things like, "You know so-and-so is moving out. She made it. She is getting out of here!" To which others would respond, "Oh, yeah? Where is she moving to?" The answer was usually a neighborhood I had never heard of before. Nevertheless, one thing I understood was that they were celebrating because someone was able to move out of what I had considered my childhood paradise.

As we got closer, my friends and I could see that the moving van was parked in front of my front door. I recognized a fire line of relatives and friends quickly tossing furniture from our apartment into the moving van. Even as kids, we had said goodbye to enough friends to know that once a moving van comes and a friend leaves, you would never see that friend again.

The night before something bad *almost happened* to me. But now, something bad *was happening* to me. I was experiencing a fear just as great as the fear I experienced when the strangers came banging on our back door. However, it was not fear of an immediate physical threat, but rather fear of the unknown. I feared what my life would be like without Michelle and Enith in it. All three of us approached my mother with tears welling in our eyes, and I told my mother that I did not want to move.

"We are moving to live with your aunt."

"Why?"

Her matter-of-fact tone came off like a plumber telling a customer what damage had been done and how it had to be fixed.

"Two men tried to kill us last night, and they will likely try it again. So before they do, we are leaving and getting away from them and the rest of these crazy black people. Now, stop crying and start helping." My greater instinct of self-preservation overshadowed the sadness of losing my friends.

Before the moving van pulled off, my mother and I went around to our friends and neighbors to say goodbye for good. Everyone was sad to see us go. However, we were congratulated on being able to move away from the crazy, violent black people who would remain amongst them after we left. For those who were not home when we left, I never got the chance to say goodbye. The bottom line was that we had to leave immediately. We had to escape my childhood paradise.

This is my first memory of associating the black people who surrounded me with something other than just being cool. Sure, if I saw a particular black person being chased by the cops, I assumed that this individual's decisions had led to actions that were deemed socially detrimental. That seemed like a simple enough reason for why he was being chased. However, I had never associated negative social behavior with black people in general.

Suddenly, negative social behavior had a broader application beyond the two black guys that tried to break into our home. This general negativity was being applied to *all those* crazy black people in the projects. From that day forward, I would notice my new association of the black identity with self-destructive social and behavioral values in my mind, within my community, and throughout American society.

Chapter 2

The University District and Hampton Elementary

In the middle of the school semester and with no idea how long our stay would be, my mom and I moved to my aunt and uncle's beautiful home in the Rosedale neighborhood, on Detroit's West Side. Rosedale, with its picturesque single-family homes made of brick and meticulously manicured front lawns, was physically nothing like the Brewster projects. But what made Rosedale really stand out were the dutifully attended-to gardens on islands of land that ran down the middle of each street in the neighborhood.

Due to our sudden arrival, I had to enroll in a small private school called DoReMe for the remainder of the second grade. Although I was made aware that we were in transition, I made it a point to make some friends at school. But within a short time, the semester ended and another celebratory moving van showed up at the front door.

My mom and I were moving to Detroit's University District, which I would soon learn was regarded as one of the best neighborhoods in Detroit.

My mother had landed a higher-paying job at the local post office, which allowed her to afford to rent a duplex at the Southwest end of the University District. Although ninety percent of the University District is made up of single-family mini-mansions, the area we moved to had several blocks of affordable duplexes. We found ourselves a new home at 17355 Warrington

Drive. Although we were on the edge of the neighborhood, we would now officially be residents of Detroit's University District.

Just a few months before our departure from the Brewsters, I was in the University District, watching my aunt getting married. I remember having a ball that day because I got to play with my new cousin—technically cousin-in-law, Kevin, who was about three years older than me. The ceremony was held in the groom's parents' lush backyard, and I marveled at the way the neighborhood bore the same bounty and promise. Thinking of it as I unpacked my things, I was thrilled to realize that we now lived there, too.

The University District was so unlike the Brewster Projects that it may as well have been on a different planet. There were tall, beautiful, mature trees everywhere. All of the lots had plenty of space, and every family had a huge brick home with impeccably maintained front lawns and spacious backyards. A typical house there was built sometime in the 1920s and 1930s and had two stories, a basement, and four to six bedrooms. Stained glass windows were so typical that they could barely be considered an amenity. Many houses had parallel staircases, separated by a wall, which would lead to the same place. The stairs were built with the intention that one set would be for the homeowners and the other for their servants. Though the same stairs were not used that way anymore, the wall served as a reminder of the rigidity of the class structure that once ruled the District. But to a seven-year-old kid, they were just two sets of stairs going to the same place.

My new in-laws' place was a three-story, six-bedroom, Tudor-style home with a finished basement, a long driveway that ran up the side of the house, and a backyard with a spacious two-car garage. Like countless other homes in the neighborhood, the garage had a basketball rim attached to it. How revolutionary this was to a kid from the projects! It meant that even if you sucked at basketball, you still got to play. The main competition would often be a tired dad who had just arrived home from work.

Our new home on Warrington Drive was a very nice duplex with pinkish-red brick and a huge bay window for each of the two stories of the house. Like all the other duplexes in the neighborhood, ours had its own front yard and driveway. Lo and behold, the back door was even safe to open! It led to our very own back porch, which looked out onto our very own backyard.

The University District was bordered to the west by a street called Livernois Avenue, which was nicknamed the Avenue of Fashion. There were shoe stores, clothing stores, even a shop that exclusively sold fur coats. There were no penny candy stores like in the Brewsters on Livernois, but there were several grocers, ice cream parlors, and a huge car dealership. In addition to retail, there were pharmacies, family-owned restaurants, accounting offices, and the private practices of local dentists and doctors.

But I immediately missed the atmosphere of my old neighborhood. The Brewsters had a *pulse*. Good or bad, there was always some commotion. All day and far into the night, there would be kids causing a ruckus, adults yelling, cop cars patrolling, and sirens blaring. Lots of people would stay home all the time talking, laughing, drinking, playing cards, or just partying out front. There were always able-bodied people, many of them grown men, hanging around without purpose, watching others go off to work.

In the University District, my block was peaceful during the day and eerily quiet at night. Parents expected their kids to be home before the streetlights came on in the evening, and kids understood that they had better do so. About half of the residents on my block and the adjacent blocks were black, but no one stood around on corners talking all day long. There was no drinking or singing in public. When adults hung out, it was in their own backyards and primarily on the weekends. On weekdays, husbands went to work, mothers ran errands, and kids went to school and participated in extracurricular activities. People of every age seemed to have goals that they were always working towards. Compared to the projects, there was more intensity in the air. There was an apparent need for people to take care of things.

Besides our immediate neighbors, those living in the University District's mini-mansions seemed to be economically homogenous—the same way the residents in the Brewsters were economically homogenous. However, the University district was far more racially diverse and affluent. As far as I could tell, it was about 70 percent white and 25 percent black, with the remaining five percent not quite fitting into either category. The overwhelming majority of its homeowners were professionals: doctors, lawyers, accountants, and business owners.

At that time, I perceived my new life in the University District as neither good nor bad, but simply as something new. I did not yet comprehend how truly fortunate I had become.

It was at this time in my life that I began to grasp the complexity of the terms *rich* and *poor*. A few days after we moved in, my mother bought a new car. That afternoon, I accompanied my Mom on a drive to an adjacent neighborhood called Palmer Woods, feeling every bit like a new millionaire.

Palmer Woods borders two other very affluent neighborhoods, Sherwood Forest and the Detroit Golf Club Estates. Palmer Woods, Sherwood Forest, and the Golf Club Estates were neighborhoods composed entirely of mansions, some as large as thirty thousand plus square feet.

My mom and I drove Palmer Woods's winding, labyrinthine roads, and I gazed, genuinely awestruck, into the beams of sunshine that pierced through the canopy of tree branches that hung over the streets. I only knew that I had not died and gone to heaven because the streets were not paved with gold.

Seeing that level of affluence up close took the concept of wealth, for me, out of the realm of black-and-white television fantasy. It was now as real as the people smelling their roses as we rode past. Upon returning home and back down to earth, I was no longer ignorant to the reality of rich and poor.

Chapter 3

The Emergence of Two Societies

While I had grown fond of my new life in the University District, I was really missing my friends Michelle and Enith. None of the friends that I made at DoReMe lived in the University District. As I had with my friends in the Brewsters, I understood that I would likely never see them again.

Fortunately, the entire block welcomed my mom and me with open arms, especially the Cubics, the white, Jesuit family who lived in the duplex next door. Mr. Cubic, who taught at the Jesuit school around the corner, and Mrs. Cubic, a stay-at-home mom, had two daughters and a son. On the second night in our new home, the entire Cubic family came over to welcome us to the neighborhood. Mrs. Cubic even baked an apple pie, which everyone enjoyed eating.

The eldest Cubic child, Gale, was in the sixth grade and the middle sister, Jennifer, was my age. The son, Tim, was two years younger than me. That evening, he brought over a box full of Legos, and we combined his Legos with the few that I had. We played with each other long after Tim's family returned home.

The Cubic girls were nice, but their circumspect attitude let me know right away that neither would be a substitute for Michelle. They were no Youngbloods. They were white like Michelle, but they didn't talk like

Michelle. Although Tim and I did not share the same taste in music—he and his sisters were fans of rock-and-roll—we found a ton of other common interests. Sometimes we would catch insects in jars and make them fight. Other afternoons, we'd build skateboards or go-carts. Our shared love for building stuff was the glue that easily held our friendship together.

In addition to Tim, a Peruvian kid named Juan found a spot on my roster of friends. Juan was my age, and we would be starting the third grade together in the fall at Hampton Elementary School. He lived across the street from our house with his parents and grandmother. Juan was shorter and thinner than me, with brown, curly hair that bounced when he walked. He was happy-go-lucky with a perpetually naughty grin that complimented my perpetually silly grin. Juan was the type to accept any dare. Had he known me then, he probably would have gone into that dark, creepy corridor in the Brewsters. I bet he would've gone without even being dared.

Although Juan and his family spoke Spanish and ate Peruvian food, he was just like my buddy Enith from the Brewsters when he was outside of his home. He was a youngblood through-and-through. He was my brother from another mother.

Juan introduced me to his best friends Tracy and Lacy, a pair of black twin boys. I liked them both right away. To me, they were cool personified. They were five years older than us, but sometimes their immaturity blurred our age gap. Though their worldly opinions made them seem like miniature adults to Juan and me, they were just a couple of naughty pre-teens amidst all the actual adults on our block. They were heading into the eighth grade at

Hampton Middle School on a pro-black tip that often teetered on the verge of being anti-white.

Although I didn't find anyone to replace Michelle, I had found three guys to replace Enith and had discovered a new kind of friend in Tim. When I wasn't playing with Juan, Tracy, and Lacy, I was playing with Tim. But, I soon noticed that Tim would often make excuses to go home whenever Juan came over to play and that he never played with Tracy or Lacy either. I just assumed that he was too young to play with the twins and figured that because Juan could often be hot headed, something bad had probably transpired between the two before my arrival.

Nonetheless, one day, I finally asked why Tim wasn't a member of our Warrington crew. Juan shrugged his shoulders. Tim just wasn't cool enough. The twins took the opportunity to assert that even though the Cubics acted friendly, like all white people, they didn't *really like* black people. Their analysis ignored the fact that the Cubics genuinely showed affection towards me, not to mention that such an assumption neglected to take into account that Juan was not black. Their case wasn't helped when they resorted to stating things like "I just feel that they don't like black people" and making references to the mini-series Roots.

*

Those days were my first introduction to the divide between the rich and poor. It was also my first introduction to the divide between those who identify with America's white mainstream culture and those who identify with

America's black subculture. This identification often serves as an oversimplified way for people to size one another up and self-segregate into peer groups based primarily on racial identity.

But here is where things get tricky. I have subsequently discovered that America's white mainstream culture is rooted in the principles of a free market society, one in which a person's skills, values, and social behavior take precedence over one's race. Conversely, America's black subculture is rooted in the principles of a racist society, one in which one's race takes precedence over skills, values, and social behavior.

At a very young age, I learned that in heterogeneous America, people customarily identified with either white or black culture and their representative social norms and values. What I didn't know was that in doing so, we often unknowingly choose to go through life as citizens in either a free market society in which skills, values, and social behaviors are paramount, or as citizens in a racist society which places race above everything.

In a racially homogeneous society, self-segregation would come down to shunning individuals solely by their behavior and values. Like members of a homogenous society as really young kids, ignorant to what *race* means in America, we rejected or otherwise embraced aspects of certain cultures without perceiving race as a fundamental factor. We self-segregated by shunning or gravitating towards certain skills, values, and social behaviors.

At this point, neither Michelle nor Juan had self-segregated, nor were they black by race, yet they both identified with and adopted certain aspects of what we all perceived to be cool black culture. However, as older kids, Tracy

26

and Lacy had already self-segregated and were living life as citizens in a racist society. They saw the Cubic family's supposed dislike of them as circumstantial evidence of a general racial prejudice.

The thought of their often socially harmful behavior as a possible reason for the Cubic family's supposed dislike for them did not factor into their equation. The twins never offered any direct evidence of the Cubic family's alleged racism. They just had an almost religious-like faith in the existence of racism everywhere.

At that time, I really didn't get where the twins were coming from. I was too busy trying to fit in to challenge their claims. But I thought that they had to be mistaken. Hell, why would the Cubics take the time to bake an apple pie to welcome my mom and me to the neighborhood like that if they didn't like black people? Why would they insist that I play with Tim if they didn't like black people?

From the time I was born until those early days living in the University District, my outlook on life was mercifully cushioned by my naïveté. But life in America was forcing me to become more intuitive. Soon enough, the terms race, racism, and racist would start to matter to me much in the same way that they mattered to Tracy and Lacy.

Chapter 4

The Hampton Elementary Crew vs. The Warrington Crew

Every day, Juan and I would walk to school together, but unfortunately, our classes were on completely different schedules. We didn't even see each other during lunch or recess.

Without Juan in my life during school hours, I needed to acquire a different set of friends at Hampton Elementary. The vast majority of my new classmates had been classmates since the first grade, and my newness felt conspicuous.

However, within the first few days of school, I became a member of the smart kids' group. This group of racially diverse kids would become my Hampton crew for the next three years. It consisted of two Youngbloods named John Woods and Eric Grundy and two white guys named Jeremy Silverstein and Noel Schulman, as well as two black girls: Lea Davis and Kelly Strong.

John was an all-around nice guy. He was a big boy, tall and a bit hefty. Though he knew he was smart, he was endlessly humble about it. On the other hand, Noel was just as smart and a complete self-promoter. If he owned a T-shirt with his report card printed on it, he would've proudly worn it every day.

Jeremy was very studious, easygoing, and witty, and Eric managed to pull off being very cool and funny while still hitting the books with focus and dedication. In that regard, we were practically identical. When report cards came around, our grades were even identical.

Kelly was chubby and opinionated. She actually believed that her third-grade opinion on any subject mattered and would expound her views given even the slightest opportunity.

Finally, there was the cute girl, Lea. Even though she was quiet, she somehow always managed to be in the thick of things. There were plenty of differences amongst us, but my teachers lumped me into this group of human Skittles due to my appreciation for learning. Even if we had been more or less forced into camaraderie by our teachers, I genuinely liked the other members of our group.

While I could speculate on the reasons why the other smart kids cared so much about good grades, I'm not sure if it was an appreciation for learning new things or fear of failure that motivated me to get good grades. It was easy for me to understand the immediate, sometimes physical consequences for bad grades. These consequences were belt whippings.

I had to take it on faith that good grades would afford me a better spot in the place called "adulthood," a place where I had never been but would eventually arrive. Good grades and what they could do for me in adulthood required faith the same kind of faith that went into Jesus's return. No one in my community had experienced a reality where Jesus had returned, but there were plenty of voices professing their faith in his return. On the other hand, there were plenty of voices in my community professing their faith in a reality in which good grades *would not* help them ascend in life.

The members of my new Hampton crew all had parents who were professionals and lived in mini-mansions deep inside the University District. They existed in a reality where good grades led to economic success for members of their inner circle.

Their reality minimized the need to rely on faith when it came to the future benefits of good grades because their current existence was due, in part, to their parents' decision to sacrifice present pleasures for future success in a free market society.

However, my immediate circle included voices from Tracy and Lacy who perceived society as a racist society. According to them, being black in that society meant that even though my mom and I were now living in a better neighborhood and I was attending a better school, we were still losing because we were black. However, in a free market society, we were winning.

*

The other side of the Kitchen

John, Eric, Noel, Jeremy, and I would often play after school at either Eric's or Jeremy's house. Eric had the basketball rim, and Jeremy had the mom who was always preparing something for us to eat. On one eventful day after school, we went over to Jeremy's house to play.

After a while, Jeremy's mom called us into the kitchen. Her smile told us that we were not in trouble. "Would anyone like some candy?" she asked.

30

Being that we were eight-year-olds, it was pretty much a rhetorical question. I thought to myself, Hell yeah! Luckily, good manners prevailed, and I politely replied, "Yes, please."

The others took my cue and in unison yelled, "Yes, please!"

"All right, then," Jeremy's mother said, "come on over here."

She opened a drawer that was three times as deep as any of the other drawers in the kitchen, and we all scuttled over. I poked my head forward a little to look down into the drawer. Damn! It was entirely filled with candy.

To get a glimpse of that much candy just a few months earlier, I would need to walk twenty minutes to the penny candy store from my apartment in the Brewsters. But Jeremy had access to tons of candy right there in his kitchen, with permission to get more of it any time he wanted to. Unimaginable! Not just that, but the candy drawer was located in what Jeremy called the "other" part of the kitchen. I had never lived in a house with a kitchen big enough to be divvied up into multiple zones. My kitchen had no "other" parts.

As I glanced around Jeremy's kitchen, peering once again into the seemingly bottomless drawer of candy, it occurred to me that my mom and I may have come a long way from the projects, but we were still nowhere close to these people.

Wealth and poverty are relative. When everyone around is rich, no one feels particularly rich. In a similar vein, poor people don't fully grasp their poverty until a rich guy shows up to create a contrast.

31

I never felt poor in the Brewsters because no one living there had any wealth to begin with. The neighbors we left behind in the Brewsters would not have considered us poor now that we were living in the University District. And yet, after seeing Jeremy's kitchen, I suddenly felt we were tragically poor.

Upon returning home, I thought about how Enith and Michelle were missing out. But I couldn't help but believe that my association with Jeremy would lead to a lot more candy than my association with either Enith or Michelle ever could.

If forced to choose between two groups of friends that I otherwise liked equally, my sense of self-preservation won out, and I gravitated toward those who could give me more candy.

*

Church on Sunday - Church on Saturday

I was having a blast in school. Thanksgiving came and went, and then talk of winter break was in the air.

All of the kids in my class were looking forward to Christmas vacation when they could spend time away from school, be it at home playing or traveling to visit relatives.

Before I knew it, the day before winter break arrived and we were all saying, "See you next year."

Over the break, I spent a lot of time playing with my Warrington crew. I had a great Christmas that year. There was certainly nothing to complain about.

Inevitably, winter break ended and we went back to school. With purely benign intentions, one of our teachers asked us what we did over the break. As kids, our responses mostly centered on presents we had received. I was pretty excited to get up and tell everyone about the racetrack and Legos I got. That is until Noel stood up. Here is when I found out that some of my Hampton friends were not only white but Jewish as well.

In his usual cocky way, he boasted about all the presents he got on the first night of Hanukkah, which vastly outnumbered what I had received for Christmas. But he wasn't done yet. Just when I thought I couldn't get more jealous, he talked about a second night with even more gifts, and then a third. In fact, it sounded as though he'd celebrated Christmas every single day of the winter break. Thanks to Noel, the first thing I learned about Jewish kids was that they got more than a week's worth of Christmas presents. I was incredulous! I felt cheated!

As Noel proudly described all the nights of Hanukkah, a girl a few seats behind me murmured just loud enough for the rest of the class to hear, "Hanukkah sounds better than Christmas."

Our teacher, a black woman, sensed the disgruntlement and disbelief among some of us other children. To keep the peace and turn this into a teachable moment, she enlisted Jewish kids in the class to explain their religion. The bottom line for me was that being Jewish meant getting a ton of toys over Christmas break and going to church on Saturdays.

Although I was jealous about the number of toys my Jewish friends got, I pitied the fact that they must have missed out on Saturday morning

33

cartoons. But my sympathy was short-lived when Noel declared that he typically spent less than three hours at the synagogue on Saturday. Just like that, I was stewing with envy again.

Whenever my family went to church, it seemed as if we forgot that we were supposed to leave. We spent all day and night at church on Sundays, then went again on Wednesday nights. Sometimes there was even a Friday night service. Church was like a part-time job, especially because I had to attend choir rehearsals on Wednesdays and Fridays as well. Fortunately, our choir was fantastic!

The gospel music that our choir produced could stand on its own against any world-renowned R&B act. In fact, we often competed against other choirs in what was known as "Midnight Musicals," which started at 11 PM and went on as late as 5 or 6 in the morning. Choirs would come from all over southwest Michigan, and sometimes even from out of state to sing at what we called "The Cathedral."

The Cathedral used to be a synagogue until the Jewish congregation left for another synagogue in the suburbs. It was an impressive venue. Its pews were able to seat thousands, and its choir stand must have seated over a hundred members. The music that came from those Midnight Musicals was simply legendary. Considering all of the competition, time, family, and community support that was devoted to cultivating the gospel choirs, it is easy to understand how so many great R&B artists are products of the black community and its churches. It's the same formula used to produce black NBA

34

and NFL stars. Unfortunately, this formula is seldom used to produce black engineers, doctors, or captains of industry.

*

Kevin

The school year eventually ended, and when I wasn't playing with my friends on Warrington, I was attending Vacation Bible School at my church. My grandmother would pick me up and take me there to learn about Jesus. Or, according to her, to stay off the streets, where trouble was always lurking. On one of the days that I didn't have to go to Vacation Bible School, I hopped on my bike and rode half a mile to my friend Eric's house. When I arrived, I found him and another familiar face standing in the driveway. It was my cousin Kevin, who I knew lived in the neighborhood but not exactly where. We recognized each other instantly.

My mom had promised to take me to his house one day, but that day had not arrived yet.

"What's up, Dre!" Kevin shouted as I rolled up into the driveway. He then proceeded to introduce me to Eric as though we were strangers and I had come to visit him instead.

"Yo, this is my cousin, Andre."

Eric's eyes widened. "Kevin is your cousin!" He said it as if there was some benefit to being Kevin's cousin that I was not aware of. With more pride than the situation called for, I replied, "Yeah, we're cousins. My aunt married his uncle."

Eric looked over at Kevin and explained, "Me and Andre are in the same class."

After the initial surprise of our common connection had worn off, we decided to go to Kevin's bedroom to play with his Atari game system. Video games were still a novelty at the time, so I was blown away and immediately wanted one for myself, even if it was prohibitively expensive.

My cousin Kevin seemed to be in the same socioeconomic sphere as the members of my Hampton crew. Maybe he didn't have a drawer bursting with candy, but he lived in a house the same size as my other friends, *and* he had an Atari.

Eventually, I went home after promising to return the next day and caught up with my Warrington Street crew. I related the story of finding my cousin Kevin, especially making sure to emphasize the thrill of playing Atari. Tracy looked at me strangely and asked, "Kevin on Muirland is your cousin?"

For the second time that day, and with a bit too much pride, I replied, "Yeah. Do you know him"?

"Hell yeah! Everybody knows Kevin. He's cool as hell and always has something you want. Homeboy has got *money*."

I felt as though my cousin was a celebrity.

Kevin not only had the reputation of a kid who got everything a kid could want, but he also had a reputation among the adults in my family for being very smart. He got excellent grades without even trying. In fact, I was surprised by his total indifference towards learning. As I got to know Kevin

36

better over that summer, I learned that his attitude towards academics was identical to Tracy and Lacy's—practically non-existent.

Kevin's parents apparently had faith in education, and that faith paid off in the form of a very comfortable home and lifestyle, but Kevin himself had little faith in the ways school could help him succeed.

By this time in their lives, Kevin, Tracy, and Lacy had chosen to self-segregate away from America's dominant free- market society and culture, which is all too often misrepresented and oversimplified as white culture. By conflating scholarship with white culture, they legitimized their indifference about school and the tools needed to be marketable.

That attitude was a reflection of a cultural divide that I initially thought was just between black guys like Tracy and Lacey, whose economic status put them on the periphery of the University District. However, I soon came to realize that such apathy towards scholastic achievement was not restricted to those living in multi-unit housing.

When school started up again, I was able to continue competing with the other smart kids in my class. My performance as a fourth grader was above average, both in school and on standardized tests. However, I couldn't help but wonder how much better I would have been able to perform if I had attended math camp to prepare for standardized tests like some of my Hampton friends were.

My parents may not have been in a financial position to send me to math camp, but my mom always forced me to do all of my homework when I got home from school. However, once I left my house and caught up with my

Warrington crew, thoughts of school and homework faded into the background. My parents' enthusiasm about education and my friends' indifference toward it were at constant odds pulling me in different directions, and I hadn't quite decided which side to lean into and go with.

*

Check it in homes

My fourth and fifth grade school years passed, and each summer brought about a new routine for me. My days alternately revolved around riding my bike through the neighborhood, playing football in the street with my Warrington friends, playing basketball at Eric's house, marathon-binges on video games with Kevin, and going to Vacation Bible School with my grandmother. Another routine was forming throughout the neighborhood as well: the number of white families leaving our neighborhood was swelling, while more black families were moving into the neighborhood in celebratory vans.

By the sixth grade, my school's atmosphere and culture had changed noticeably from when I arrived just three years prior. Though my Hampton crew's status as "smart kids" had not changed, our teachers were now spending more time disciplining students in the class and, consequently, less time teaching. Furthermore, the school bullies were turning into thugs with criminal rap sheets.

My Warrington crew had shifted away from indifference to outright disdain of school, from admiration of the cool to celebration of the menacing.

Respect, as would be afforded to a vicious pit bull, now came from being feared. It was sought after like gold.

Tracy and Lacy were taking on the persona of two thugs. In fact, my Warrington crew's behavior was starting to remind me of the things that I heard about and occasionally witnessed in the Brewster projects. And, as more celebratory moving vans came, so did incidents of crime. While my mother had made huge strides in trying to leave our past life in the projects behind, my Warrington crew and others were making great strides in emulating life in the projects, running towards that old, more dangerous life at full speed.

Hampton, once viewed as a safe haven, was becoming more dangerous by the day. In fact, one day after school as I waited for Juan to walk home with me, a long-time resident of the University District robbed me. He was a well-known thug in my grade named Joe Rivers, who (strangely enough) conducted his criminal enterprise from the comfort of his parent's mini-mansion.

"How much money you got on you?" he asked. His tone was oddly polite.

Regardless, I instantly knew things were bad from the three henchmen lingering behind him as his insurance just in case I was brave enough to tell him to get the hell out of my face. I was not a frail kid. Maybe that's why Joe brought backup. However, I was neither big enough nor stupid enough to single-handedly take on four guys over the paltry sixty cents I had in my pocket.

"I only have sixty cents," I replied. He extended his hand. "Check it in, homes."

I had a target on my back. From that day forward, Joe and his band of affluent hoodlums would keep an eye out for my pocket change. Inevitably, the day would come when I would not have any. With all the bravery I could muster, I said, "Here, this is all I have." I proceeded to give him my change. As I looked over his shoulders at his friends to make sure they were all listening, I added: "And that is all I will ever have for you." Nevertheless, he replied with a grin, "We'll see you tomorrow."

When Juan finally came outside, I didn't mention the incident. But, as we were walking home, I remembered that Eric once told me that Joe lived near him. Taking a chance, I jumped on my bike and rode to Kevin's house to do some research.

"Yo," I said when Kevin answered the door, getting right to the point, "Do you know a guy named Joe Rivers?"

"Yeah, I know him. He lives on the next block, but I know his older brother better. Why?"

With a bit of exaggeration, I told my story. "Yeah? Well, Joe and about seven other dudes rolled up on me talking about how they would kick my ass if I didn't give them all of my money. Of course, I couldn't take on eight guys, so I handed over the 60 cents that were in my pocket. I was thinking about getting my boys Tracy and Lacy from my block and some of their friends to help me kick their asses, but I thought I should see what you know about Joe first."

Visibly upset, Kevin replied, "What?! Oh, hell no. Joe won't be bothering you again. You'll get your money back tomorrow."

I was silent. I believed him but had no idea how he could be so sure about it.

He then added, "But when he gives it back, just say 'thanks' and walk away."

Kevin explained that Joe belonged to a gang called the 7 Mile BKs. If I fought Joe one-on-one and won, I would then have to fight the rest of the 7 Mile BKs until I inevitably lost. Even if I were Bruce Lee reincarnated, and was able to beat the whole gang by myself, they would just shoot me to ensure a victory.

"7 Mile BKs never lose. 'BK' stands for Black Killers. They will kill you over nothing, so be careful," he said.

Are you one of them?" I asked.

"No, I do my own thing," he replied proudly. "I don't need to sell drugs to get what I want. That's the reason most of those guys are in gangs. Their parents won't buy them what they want, so they sell drugs. There are a lot of BKs at Hampton Middle School, and even some, like Joe, at Hampton Elementary. You ever hear of a guy named Gill?"

I had, indeed. In fact, I'd heard about Gill since the third grade; he had *that much* of a reputation. Gill Gunn was a year ahead of me at Hampton Elementary. Once, when I was in fifth grade, he stopped me in the hallway and asked if I was a smart kid. I told him that I was a B student. He then proceeded to threaten me with an ass-kicking if his next report card was better

41

than mine. I was dumbfounded. It was the strangest threat I'd ever received. I didn't even know the guy, so why would he want to hit me upside the head if he got a better GPA than me? Why would he even care?

Luckily, several weeks later, I managed to get a better report card than Gill and survive unscathed.

"Stay away from Gill," Kevin said when I finished recounting the story of Gill's strange threat. "He's the type who shoots first and won't ask questions later."

The next day it went down just like Kevin said it would. Joe found me outside the school in the same spot. He returned my 60 cents with a simple, "Thanks, homes." I responded likewise as Kevin instructed me to, and he never bothered me again.

*

First last dance

Despite constantly having to avoid hoodlums at school, I still managed to enjoy life at Hampton Elementary. I took pleasure in making pottery in art class, playing the trumpet in music class, and horsing around in gym class. But, the school dance, one of the last events of the sixth grade and a milestone in the journey towards puberty, caused some internal conflict for me.

According to my church, God did not look favorably upon listening and dancing to secular music. I was concerned that some in my church would consider a school dance as state-sponsored sinning. I justified going to the dance by telling myself that I was still too young for my sins to count, and it was just a rite of passage, anyway.

I had a game plan, too. I would sin as little as possible, just enough to have fun—but not so much that it might count against me with the man upstairs. That meant no dancing. Instead, I would strategically stand on the perimeter telling jokes with John, who I figured would not be eager to strut his stuff on the dance floor.

The school decked out the gym, where the dance would be held for a quick hour and a half. It looked like a high school prom, with streamers and banners and an actual DJ. At one corner of the gym, there were a few tables and chairs for the teachers to sit at and monitor carefully where the boys were placing their hands.

At the beginning of the dance, the principal got up and said a few words about growing up and leaving elementary school. Over at their lookout, our teachers seemed genuinely emotional about us graduating, but none of the kids appeared to care. The girls were too focused on getting asked to dance, and guys were even more nervous about asking. A few of the better dancers were shuffling with impatience, eager to show off their dance skills. I just wanted the entire thing to be over.

The dance started with a crowd-pleasing Earth, Wind & Fire song, followed up by some Michael Jackson, the Eurythmics, and The Police. I noticed some girls were asking guys to dance. I had not prepared myself for this contingency when I formulated my game plan, so I tried to make myself small next to John in the hope that some ugly girl would not ask me to dance. The worst thing would be to waste my sinning dancing with an ugly girl.

I spent the majority of the dance making John and a few other wallflowers laugh, watching the clock out of the corner of my eye. Eventually, the DJ announced that he was playing the last song. I was almost in the clear when, out of nowhere, my teacher Mrs. Felton approached.

"Have you two danced yet?" she asked.

"No, ma'am, but, um…we're okay and … " John stammered. "Well, this is a dance, and you need to dance with someone."

It was an order. My game plan was out the window. Mrs. Felton was about to force me down the road to eternal damnation. As she scanned the gymnasium for a couple of girls that she could demand that we invite to dance, I silently explained to Jesus that I really did not want to dance and hoped that he wouldn't mark this one down as a sin.

Mrs. Felton pointed John towards a very quiet girl in our class named Michelle Silverman. I knew that if I didn't find a dance partner immediately on my own, Mrs. Felton would surely find one for me. I couldn't decide what was worse: Jesus seeing me dance or my friends seeing Mrs. Felton pairing me off with an ugly girl. As I frantically bargained with Jesus to just spare me the whole thing, my friend Lea came up and happily asked me to dance. *Thank you*, God!

I thought this was divine salvation until I realized that I had no idea how to dance with a girl. We stood in front of each other for an eternity before the song started. Lea must have noticed that I was nervous because she leaned in and said, "Andre, relax. It's just dancing." She just as well could have said, "Relax, Judas. Just take the silver."

The song was "Time Won't Give Me Time" by Culture Club, and I was easily able to find the groove. Lea and I slowly rocked and swayed just as if we were in the church choir. Once my nervousness gave way to contentment, and then to joy, it occurred to me: *Hey, dummy, Lea asked you to dance. Maybe she likes you.* Just as I started hoping the song would go on for a few more minutes, it began to fade out. The name of the song couldn't have been more fitting.

During lunch on our last day of school, my class and several other classes, as per usual, were sitting on the gymnasium floor with our legs folded while being watched by the vice principal. It was the last time we would sit and wait to be lead into the lunchroom to eat lunch at Hampton Elementary.

Normally, the only thing that the vice principal would say to us during this time was, "Be quiet." But on that particular day, he broke into what could be considered a graduation speech. With an uncharacteristic amount of affection, he assured us that we would be missed. He went on to say that even though Hampton Middle School was physically attached to Hampton Elementary, we would be entering a very different environment. He commanded us to stay focused on our studies reassuring us of the value of an excellent education. Like many adults in my life, he insisted that academic rigor was the key to success in that place called adulthood. Finally, with optimism in his voice, he said: "I wish you all the best."

45

What do you call a black doctor in Virginia?

Summer vacation was in full swing. I was constantly having fun, playing football in the streets, basketball in someone's backyard, or video games at my cousin Kevin's house. Although Juan and I were still thick as thieves, and I was still hanging out with Tim next door, my interactions with Tracy and Lacy were slowly dissipating. On the rare occasion that I was in their presence, they were far from the happy and carefree guys they once were. My cool, pro-black, Youngbloods had turned into pro-black, anti-white street thugs. They called themselves *"real niggas"*—the expression like a trademark authenticating their new black identity.

While we played street football, Tracy would give us black history lessons between downs like a football coach yelling out plays. He had a very attentive audience. Juan and I still looked up to Tracy and Lacy, as if they were ambassadors from that foreign land called adulthood. Tracy didn't paint a pretty picture of the place, either.

In fact, adulthood seemed like a cliff we couldn't save ourselves from driving over. It was a dark place where bad things happened to black people. He described our future just as Black History Month painted our past: black victims forced to struggle against our white victimizers, dealing endlessly with systemic racism. My black identity went from being a member of a cool people who survived slavery, overturned Jim Crow laws, and won the fight for civil rights, to one of being thugs and perpetual victims.

Tracy and Lacy continually cited circumstantial evidence of whites' dislike or hatred of blacks by saying things like, "They are only moving out of the neighborhood because more blacks are moving in."

They seemed to have a valid point. Over the course of three years, the majority of the residents in the University District had gone from white to black. It seemed to be a daily occurrence to find out that, just like the businesses that were leaving the Avenue of Fashion, more of my white schoolmates, including Noel and Jeremy, were leaving the neighborhood.

"Yeah, they integrated the schools. But the first chance they get, the whites just move away," they'd say. Or, "It's racism! You think you are going to get a job over a white man? Nigga, please!" Tracy and Lacy's perspective on our society was slowly eroding my faith in education as a means to socio-economic ascension and well-being.

"What do they call a black doctor in Virginia? A Nigga." Tracy would proclaim. The twins were describing a society in which an uneducated, unemployed convicted white pedophile, casually enjoying an incestuous relationship with his daughter, is more valued than one of the remaining black doctors in our neighborhood.

*

Middle School

The first day of middle school was on one of those late summer days where you could feel a hint of autumn's arrival in the air and see the trees just beginning to change color.

47

Juan's parents decided to save up some money and send him to the Jesuit middle school around the corner where Mr. Cubic taught. Apparently, there were too many bad influences in his life at Hampton Elementary. So I walked into middle school for the first time a solo act.

At the front of the school, hundreds of students were gathered about and talking. I immediately noticed that all of them were black. On top of that, I only recognized a few of them.

Most of the kids seemed to know each other already. I was in the same neighborhood and, technically, in the same building that I had been in just a few months prior, but the makeup of this student body was drastically different now.

I spotted Lea talking to a group of cute girls in a circle. As I headed in her direction, I noticed a bunch of boys hovering around their circle like vultures. I had to dip and dodge around them to reach Lea within her circle of friends. When I mentioned that I did not recognize anyone, she informed me that we were the only members of my former Hampton crew that would be attending Hampton Middle School. In fact, a majority of Hampton's sixth graders had gone on to attend middle school elsewhere. She was considerate enough to introduce me to her cute associates, but that was little consolation for the fact that I was basically a stranger at my own school.

The bell rang, and I went to homeroom, where the sea of unfamiliar faces was narrowed down to a pond of strangers. But, as fate would have it, there was one student I recognized: Keith Reynolds. He was a big, heavy-set guy, and had been a well-known bully at Hampton Elementary. Although he was not as menacing as Gill Gunn, he was much bigger than Joe Rivers, who threatened me out of my change.

Up until now, I had avoided interaction with Keith like the plague. But now, that was going to be a lot harder to do. The teacher had assigned our seats and placed me directly behind Keith. Homeroom met twice a day, and this meant that I would spend at least two sessions per day just over the shoulder of a notorious bully.

The day had only just begun, and I already thought it couldn't get any worse. But the bad news just kept coming. Our class alternated between different classrooms to learn from different teachers and, in every single class, my seat assignment was within arm's reach of Keith.

Compared to when I first arrived at Hampton Elementary, there was a huge difference in teachers' attitudes toward students. Mrs. Felton had been a legendary disciplinarian at Hampton Elementary, but she was exceptional only because the other teachers were not nearly as stern. At Hampton Middle School, *all of the teachers* came out *swinging*. Right out of the gate, they made threats about what would happen if we did not follow the rules, which were explained in excruciating detail and peppered with threats of expulsion. After hearing all this over and over, after a time, I began to feel less like a student and more like an inmate.

By the end of the school day, I had a pretty good idea of why we were warned over and over again. The student body was just plain rowdy and lacked any desire to learn. From the get-go, Keith distinguished himself as one of the rowdiest. He disturbed the class by talking out of turn, cracking jokes, and teasing other students—and it just so happened that he decided to try to ingratiate himself with me. Self-preservation told me that it was better to let him talk to me than to risk making an enemy of him, so pretty soon we were both talking out of turn, cracking jokes, and teasing classmates.

Soon, I began to see Keith in an entirely different light. The guy that I feared to be a big bully was just a class clown. He wasn't the type to start fights, just finish them. I was surprised to discover that I had begun to consider him a friend by science class, our last subject of the day.

There, our fun resulted in Keith getting suspended from school. I had more finesse than Keith, so every time Mrs. Williams whirled her face around from the chalkboard, Keith was the only one caught with his mouth open. As a result, he was suspended the very first day of school.

While Keith enjoyed his three-day vacation, I enjoyed spreading my brand of dry humor throughout our class. I quickly became friends with Michael Green and Marvin Miller. Michael was slender, with a dark complexion. Marvin was short, with eyelids that hung unusually low over his eyes, making him look as if he was always half asleep.

When Keith returned to school, we picked up where we left off. Keith would say something to make me laugh, and I would return the favor. By the end of Keith's first day back, I had a new Hampton crew that consisted of Michael, Marvin, and Keith.

Unlike my previous crew at Hampton Elementary, my new crew could not have cared less about what was being taught in class. Our only ambition was to see if we could get one another sent to the principal's office or suspended from school.

Michael, Marvin, and I managed to get Keith suspended from school well past the three-strike maximum that first year, but his mother somehow persuaded the principal not to expel him altogether from Hampton. Expulsion would mean he would have to transfer to another school, and we would miss out on getting him into even more trouble. So we were happy that this never happened—amazingly enough.

But getting Keith suspended from school so many times was not without repercussions for us as well. Since he had destroyed his credibility with the teachers, they never believed him when he claimed to be the victim of harassment. As payback, his modus operandi was to embarrass us amongst our peers and strangers, and he perfected the art of embarrassment by ambush.

One day, I had to take the city bus somewhere after school, and Keith walked with me to the bus stop. It was unusually hot that day, so the bus arrived with all of its windows open for ventilation. Keith waited until I got on the bus, paid my fare, and started walking to my seat before yelling from outside of the bus "Yo, Dre!" He made it sound like it was an emergency. Everyone turned and stared out the windows. "Yo, Andre!" he called again. Once I scrambled to a window, he yelled at the top of his lungs, "Wear some deodorant tomorrow! It's a shame someone can come to school smelling so funky!"

Everyone on the bus, even an old lady, started laughing. Well played Keith. I just hung my head and laughed along with everyone else as the bus started moving.

*

Kids and Consequences

I spent the seventh grade being embarrassed by Keith and trying to avoid traps laid by friends trying to get me suspended from school. Keith, Michael, and Marvin were all suspended at least once, but I never was. I even got away with playing lookout while Keith stole a beautifully hand-drawn picture of Bruce Lee, donated to the school by a former student, that hung on the wall in front of the principal's door in the Administration office.

Despite my exploits, my teachers saw me as a good kid who got decent grades. They thought the three bad apples were just influencing me, and that I was otherwise a non-threat. Unlike my elementary school teachers, who expected and even demanded that I perform at a high level academically, my middle school teachers' expectations were so low that just being a non-threat won accolades.

We were still kids, but the consequences of our actions were becoming more and more severe. Fistfights now required the attention of the police. Kids were being arrested for selling drugs. Simultaneously, we were replacing our faith in education with the belief that racism would undo all the rewards that usually come with academic achievement and good social

52

behavior anyway. Why sacrifice present pleasure for future success if you are going to still be black anyway?

Around the first week of November, I noticed that I had not seen Lea in the hallways for a while. I asked Keith if he knew Lea. "Yeah," he said. "She lives a few blocks away from me." They had known one another their entire lives. Apparently, she had gotten fed up with his horsing around and hadn't been talking to him recently. He suggested that she may have transferred to another school. Keith's conjecture was certainly plausible, and I figured it might, unfortunately, be true.

After Thanksgiving break, Keith ran up to me in the hall with a look of panic on his face. Right away I was on guard for some kind of practical joke he had cooked up over the break.

"I gotta tell you something," he whispered frantically. "Lea is pregnant." I wanted to call him on his lie, but the despair in Keith's eyes hit me hard. With a steady stream of students walking past, I blurted out, "She'll be a mom before we're eighth graders?"

I felt like my childhood crush died and was replaced with someone's mother. She would no longer be the sweet little girl I had danced with at the end of elementary school. Keith and I could barely talk about it, we were so shaken. It was an aberration for a preteen girl to get pregnant, but I was particularly saddened because to me, she wasn't just some black statistic no one is ever shocked by on the news—she was my *friend*. Who is to say when you are prepared for adulthood? But I knew, even then, a child bearing a child with no marketable skills in a free market society is ill equipped for successful participation in that society.

*

Reputation matters

By the winter break, I had lost all interest in learning. Though my behavior was relatively good, compared to that of the really crazy black kids in my school, what I didn't know yet is that my once-spotless reputation would soon be tarnished.

As all of my classmates simultaneously rushed into the narrow hallway that led to Mrs. Nash's English class, Keith got sandwiched between a girl named Robin in front of him and me behind him. I decided to get Keith in trouble by grabbing Robin's butt and making it look like Keith did it. We had both grabbed her butt several times before and always got repaid with a mere punch in the chest. Why should now be any different?

Halfway through the packed passageway, I grabbed Robin's butt. Instead of turning around and hitting Keith as expected, she yelled, "Stop feeling on my butt, boy!" Keith laughed and gave me a congratulatory grin over his shoulder for the butt-grab. Unfortunately, Mrs. Nash heard Robin and flashed a look of disgust in our direction. Although she heard things like that every day from junior high school kids at the mercy of their hormones, there must have been something going on in her life that day because she really put some thought into finding out who the real culprit was.

54

After everyone sat down, Mrs. Nash calmly rose from her desk and asked Robin to stand up. The class came to a standstill. It was so quiet that I could hear my own heart thumping in my chest. Then the hammer dropped. "Which one of these boys did you let feel on your butt?" she asked in skeptical tone with an emphasis on "let." It was brilliant on her part. She had insinuated that Robin was a slut rather than a victim. She knew that Robin would feel indignant and emphatically assert her victimhood.

With her neck snapping from side to side and her hands on her hips, she retorted, "I didn't let Keith feel on my butt."

"I didn't do that," Keith protested, "Andre did it!"

I felt the entire class's eyes upon me but kept my mouth shut. "Is that true, Robin? Did Andre grab your butt?" Mrs. Nash probed.

"I thought it was Keith, but I'm not sure."

I could have easily insisted that Keith was guilty because Mrs. Nash was already inclined to see him as the culprit anyway. But grabbing a girl's butt, although commonplace around Hampton Middle School, was a very serious offense. Keith would have had to tell his parents that he got suspended not for being a class clown but for being a pervert.

Even though we routinely tried to get each other suspended from school, I considered Keith a very close friend. This would be outside the scope of tacit consent. Declining to implicate Keith one way or the other, I simply replied, "It wasn't me either." We were both sent to the principal's office. My luck had run out. Keith was really pissed at me. He was again about to be suspended from school, and he would have to face the wrath of his mother. I was terrified. I had never been in trouble, and now I would be labeled a pervert. As Keith and I walked the empty hallways toward the principal's office, I searched my brain for a way out of the mess I got us into.

I hit upon what I believed to be a plausible lie. Keith would take the fall and admit that he hit Robin on the butt, but only as a consequence of me "unintentionally" knocking his hand into her butt due to the stampede of students rushing through the passageway. Keith immediately said that it was not good enough. I thought about it for a moment and agreed.

We would need to cast some of the blame on Mrs. Nash. I suggested we could say that when Mrs. Nash asked Robin to stand up in front of the class and defend her virtue, it naturally led Robin to play the victim. If Mrs. Nash had pulled Robin aside and discreetly asked what happened, Robin would have said it was not intentional. After all, there was a lot of pushing and shoving going on inside the corridor.

"How do you know Robin would say that?" Keith asked. "She won't if we don't persuade her to say it for us. We just have to talk to Robin before we see the principal."

That meant we had to roam the halls until class was over, so we ducked and dodged the hall monitors like a pair of spies for forty minutes. When English class let out, we ran to Robin and begged her to go along with our plan with the promise of food and money in return. After she magnanimously agreed, Keith and I ran to the principal's office. As we waited to be called in, we sat directly under the empty space on the wall where the Bruce Lee picture once hung.

Keith needed no introduction, but the principal had no clue of who I was. After I had introduced myself, we told him who sent us and why. Not missing a beat, I proceeded with my opening arguments with the zeal of a defense attorney. Mr. Townson listened to all of the details that Keith and I had premeditated, including the brazen incrimination of Mrs. Nash. I especially emphasized that Keith had done nothing wrong. Mr. Townson looked at me blankly and then frowned at Keith. Despite his expression, he seemed to be buying the bullshit I was selling. Then, he told us to step outside his office and wait. We returned to the scene of our previous crime and took our seats. Keith thought it mostly went well, except that I should have also told Mr. Townson to ask Robin. I explained that I wanted Mr. Townson to ask her without our suggestion so that it would make her sound more credible.

Mrs. Nash eventually arrived and went straight to the principal's office without looking at us. After about five minutes, we were called back in.

"Keith and Andre," Mr. Townson declared. The room was thick with the kind of tension you'd expect before the verdict of a triple-homicide. "You are both being suspended."

Together, we cried out, "We didn't do anything!"

As usual, I arrived home before my mother and had plenty of time to stew about the mess I was in. When she finally returned from work, she told me that a guy she was dating from church was coming by for dinner. Before I could say anything, she immediately sent me to the store with a list of items to buy. When I got back home from the store my mom's date had already arrived. He was a cool guy named Lee. My mother was happy around him, so he was okay with me. I just could not bring myself to tell her that I had been suspended. Reasoning that it would be inappropriate to ruin the positive mood, I decided it would be best to tell her after Lee left.

As we ate dinner, my mother asked how my day went at school. Attempting to keep calm and put an end to the conversation as quickly as possible, I responded, "Oh, it went ok."

"Oh yeah? Did you learn something interesting today?" Lee blurted out, apparently wanting to demonstrate his interest in me. The banter continued for a couple of minutes, staying on school no matter how desperately I attempted to steer us towards a different topic. Just when I thought I couldn't hold out any longer, I was literally saved by the bell when the phone started ringing from the other room.

"I'll get it," I exclaimed as I jumped up from the dining table. I dashed into the living room and picked up the phone, ready to thank whoever it was that had called and rescued me.

"Hello. Davis residence. Who's speaking?"

"This is Mrs. Nash," said the voice on the other line. I nearly fainted. "Andre, is that you?"

I managed to reply, "Yes."

"Is your mother home?"

I could not believe that Mrs. Nash would suspend me and then add insult to injury by personally calling my house. My decision to postpone telling my mom was backfiring. I had wanted to tell my version of the story to my mother preemptively, but instead, she was about to hear the perverted tale directly from Mrs. Nash.

Left to my own devices, I tried to negotiate. "My mother is having dinner with company right now," I pleaded quietly, hoping she would not hear and come in from the dining room. Whispering into the receiver, I anxiously explained, "I haven't had a chance to tell her about what happened today."

"Well, can I please talk to her?"

"Um…"

"Andre, I need to tell your mother that you *have not* been suspended after all. I also want to talk to her about you and the friends you are hanging around."

All that registered in my mind was that she had bought the bullshit I sold and I could go back to school without telling my mother that I was a pervert. I told Mrs. Nash to wait a moment and ran into the dining room to tell my mother that my English teacher wanted to speak with her. Although a horrible situation had just gotten a lot better, I could not be certain I was totally out of the woods.

As my mother listened politely to Mrs. Nash, I tried to read the emotions flashing over her face: surprise at first, then disappointment, anger, relief, pride, concern, and finally understanding. Mrs. Nash said that because I was a good student and did not really cause much trouble, it would not be fair to punish me by requiring me to stay out of school and fall behind in class. Keith, on the other hand, was such a troublemaker that she needed a break from him. He would remain suspended.

59

"He's a bad influence," Mrs. Nash told my mother, "and he's bound to get your son into real trouble one day."

*

Life for the non-exceptionable

With summer vacation came more celebratory vans. But my desire and drive to learn anything written in books had already long disappeared.

With seventh grade over, I was able to hang out with Juan more. On rare occasions, I would run into Tracy and Lacy, who were now selling drugs and sometimes even using them. The twins seemed to be trying to attend every party in the Detroit area. Since I had met them, they had turned into the aimless guys that I used to see in the projects. From the way they dressed to their mannerisms, everything about them screamed, "I'm a thug." Not, "I'm cool."

I constantly heard the message that Tracy and Lacy subscribed to: our racial identity came with a stigma of inferiority and victimization that education could not resolve. However, if you were exceptionally rich and famous, you could shed the stigma placed upon the black identity. Unfortunately, none of us were exceptional in any way.

The requirement of being exceptional just to be considered the equivalent of an ordinary white American is nothing new for blacks in America. This reality was codified in the law that Homer Plessey violated on June 7, 1892. The law no longer required this exceptionalism but the racist society still required it from blacks.

60

The law at the center of the Homer Plessey case made it criminal to just be black in certain places. The place Homer Plessey's blackness was deemed criminal was in a certain compartment of a commuter train. Plessey fought the legitimacy of the law in court. However, the highest court in the land upheld the law under the doctrine of separate but equal. The Court's ruling allowed for the continued criminalization of being black.

However, there was an exception to the law that Plessey violated and it stated: "Nothing in this act shall be construed as applying to nurses attending children of the other race." Thus, a black person needed a qualifier not to be deemed a criminal and to simply enjoy privileges that whites took for granted. Imagine a reality where, in certain places, the law regards something beyond one's control, like height or sex, as criminal, and used that quality to subject certain people to criminal sanctions and the social stigma of being a criminal.

Thankfully, the Civil Rights Movement overturned such racial discriminatory laws. But for those blacks and whites who view America as a purely racist society, the necessity of a Plessey qualification still exists.

Without being exceptional in any way, Tracy and Lacy were pissed. Being an auto worker, scientist, doctor, or lawyer would not afford them the lifestyle of the exceptionally rich and famous nor guarantee them the prosperity of the average white person—but the exceptional material gains—and exceptionally easy gains, of the average drug dealer began to look like an appealing alternative.

Tracy and Lacey were still on the pro-black tip, but they put conversations about racial injustice on the back burner for talks about selling drugs, as well as the material goods and sex that came with the drug game. They were superstars, in a very small world. By the end of that summer, I could say that two members of my Warrington crew had turned from cool, pro-black Youngbloods to hardened criminals who sold drugs to their black brothers and sisters.

Juan and I *could no*t follow in their footsteps. We had become spectators staring upon their world like bystanders on a corner noticing the first indications of a fatal car accident.

*

The BK Beat down

"In those places where the rich and powerful are assembled together the weak and the indigent feel themselves oppressed by their inferior condition. Unable to perceive a single chance of regaining their equality, they give up to despair, and allow themselves to fall below the dignity of human nature."   *- Democracy in America, Alexis de Tocqueville*

The first day of eighth grade was much better because I was no longer a stranger. Now, I was a veteran evaluating all the new rookies coming to my school. Despite my new status, Lea's continued absence reminded me that my childhood friend had thrust herself into adulthood inadequately prepared. I couldn't shake the thought of that.

Keith, Michael, Marvin, and I started the eighth grade the way we left off in the seventh: with no interest in education. The days came and went. There were the random yet familiar fights in the halls, puppy love in the air, and tales of gunshots. There was also something new called "rap battles." All told, the eighth grade was nearly identical to the seventh, with the addition of one exceptional event.

On some otherwise uneventful day, I got wind of a rumor that a member of a gang known as the 8 Mile Sconies was coming to Hampton to pick up his little sister. He and his sister apparently lived in the very affluent neighborhood of Sherwood Forest. By the end of the day, I found out that there were more members of the 7 Mile BKs among my peers in school than I had previously realized.

One was Joseph Gardener, a well-known thug at Hampton Middle School that everybody called JoJo. My interactions with JoJo were always pleasant; we would occasionally crack jokes in the hall or comment on girls that crossed our path. As the end of the school day neared, the guy from the 8 Mile Sconies came to Hampton with two of his friends. They arrived before the last bell and stood across the street from the main entrance. The second the bell rang, it seemed as if the entire student body stampeded the doors to get a look at the trespassers. The sister, a girl I did not know, ran out to meet the three guys first, closely followed by a brigade of 7 Mile BKs. Behind them, the rest of the student body jockeyed for a good position to see the highly-anticipated fight.

The trespassers must have drunk a cup of courage that morning. Their first reaction was to stand their ground. Soon a mob of BKs was surrounding them. A guy right next to Keith and I threw the first punch. Before the Sconie could react, more punches and kicks came flying at him and his two associates. Despite being heavily outnumbered, they attempted to fight back. The Sconie's sister screamed in horror as it became evident that a full-blown beat-down was underway. Like blood-thirsty fans at a Roman colosseum, the crowd cheered on the 7 Mile BKs, valiantly protecting their turf from a fictitious threat.

The 8 Mile Sconies gave up the fight and headed back towards 8 Mile Road, but they were cut off by a car that came flying around the corner to the cheers of some in the crowd. At that point, it was clear that the BKs had premeditated an ambush.

The trespassers decided to split up. The guy who had come to pick up his sister got caught and beaten down between two parked cars on Margareta Avenue. One of his friends ran in a panic straight into the traffic on Livernois Avenue and was hit by a car. As he was writhing and groaning in pain, JoJo caught up with him and stomped the kid's teeth out as he lay on the pavement.

The other kid ran down an alley, only to be trailed by the BK guy driving the car. We heard the car screech to a halt at the alley's entrance, followed by the sound of a gunshot ringing out. Keith and I ran to get a better look at our classmate's brother. He was trapped in between two cars, being punched and stomped nearly to death.

The sister continued screaming frantically—her cries were almost drowned out by the cheers of our classmates watching the beating. A kid was jumping from the hood of a car onto her brother's chest and face. Keith and I looked on in bewilderment.

For some time after the guy lost consciousness, the Sconie continued getting pummeled. The mayhem was finally broken up by the blare of sirens, sending everyone scattering. I had run out of school expecting to see a garden variety fist fight, and ended up being a witness to attempted murder.

After returning home that day, I could not stop thinking about the pandemonium I witnessed. I had always known there was no shortage of hoodlums at school, but I realized that evening that I was among actual criminals every single day. I suddenly felt a great empathy for the teachers, and I suddenly understood for the first time why they acted as if we were inmates in a prison. I could also see why we were held to such low academic and social standards.

The next day in school, we heard about the life-threatening injuries sustained by the girl's brother and his friends at the hands of her own schoolmates and their friends. A morbidly detailed account of broken ribs and limbs, cracked skulls, concussions, even an eye hanging from the socket, as well as other gruesome injuries were read out over the PA system, followed by a plea for information about the perpetrators.

*
Worthless

I could understand why poor people in the projects, who thought that they had no prospects of getting ahead in life, would turn to a life of crime. But these affluent black kids were far removed from that characterization.

The Seven Mile BKs and the Eight Mile Sconies lived comfortable lives and had every advantage that proponents of equal rights and equal opportunity had fought and died for. The bitter sermons from the twins coupled with calls for restitution and reparations from Post-Civil Rights Era black politicians and social activists were assailing my eardrums constantly. However, those voices were quick to brush aside the individual choices that went into my black peers' socially deviant behavior.

Instead, those voices just blamed every negative thing in the black community on the effects of slavery or the omnipresent influence of systemic racism. The truth is that there were no Klansman urging those kids to fight. In fact, I'm pretty sure that those brave black kids who were first integrated into white schools didn't join gangs called Black Killers.

Instead of refuting the historical narrative of racism, that black people were inherently inferior, my peers were constantly attaching negative social behavior and values to our racial identity.

There was a gravitation towards social behaviors and values that were in direct contradiction to a successful existence in a free market society. More importantly, these negative social behaviors and values did nothing to eliminate the stigma placed upon black people—in fact, they only reinforced it. Those voices of racial inequality and victimization, coupled with an affection for bad social behavior and values, were coating my own still-fragile and not-yet-fully-formed black identity like tar.

I hold no grudge against Joe Rivers, the guy who robbed me of my lunch money when we were kids. Hopefully, he is an upstanding citizen, a successful father, and some kind of professional today.

However, if he stayed on the road he was traveling, he may have shared the same fate as Gill Gunn, who was convicted of killing two people over drugs before reaching the tender age of 22. Or, Joseph "JoJo" Gardner, who ended up on the TV show *America's Most Wanted* for murder and was ultimately executed by the State of South Carolina.

I'm sure that JoJo bought into the common narrative that white people were responsible for his shortcomings. In fact, he and some friends carried out a New Year's resolution to rape and kill a white woman as retribution for four hundred years of racial oppression. Years later, when I heard the news, I was not shocked at neither Gill's nor JoJo's demise. I was just saddened by the waste of potential.

*

My circle of friends in elementary school was racially diverse, united by our shared goal to succeed in learning. Our parents and teachers expected nothing less because they believed that excellence in academics was a necessity for successful participation in a free market society.

67

In those early years, we did not attribute this expectation of academic excellence to any particular race or culture. However, I was starting to hear more and more divisive voices within the black community attaching the plight of blacks solely to a victimizing white culture.

Sadly, just like Tracy, Lacy, and Kevin, many of my friends and I were beginning to equate academic excellence with that victimizing white American culture; in effect, granting white America a copyright on what it takes to be successful in a free market society. My black identity made it difficult to purchase that license.

It was nearly impossible to accept the values, social behaviors, and skills needed to be successful in a free market society because these things were now seen as belonging to our victimizers. Our priorities were shifting away from obtaining skills needed to be successful in a free market society to just being victims of a racist society.

When white and black professionals began leaving the University District, they were taking their values of success, ones divorced from race, with them as well. Hampton Middle School once had a reputation for being an institution of high academic achievement. That reputation was earned by the efforts of parents, teachers, and students and perpetuated by faith in the ability of scholastic success to influence upward mobility. It was inevitable that the school's reputation would suffer as the local residents began to lose that faith.

Those Seven Mile BKs and Eight Mile Sconies were kids who, with modest effort, probably had an above-average chance of becoming educated professionals. Nevertheless, they were cavalier towards the risk of

68

incarceration and indifferent to educational opportunities, which significantly diminished their standing in society and future earning potential. That beat-down was the violent manifestation of a broader pathology infecting the young people in my community. It was an expression of an unshakeable hopelessness in those who could see no way to become equal to their white counterparts.

In 1992, Andrew Hacket did a social experiment in which white people were asked how much in money they would want in return for living as a black individual in society. The answer was fifty-million dollars or one million dollars for each black year. These affluent black kids and other black kids in the early eighties saw their lives valued at a negative fifty-million dollars. In other words, worthless.

Chapter 5

High School: The First Clash of Societies

Hampton Middle School only went up to the eighth grade. There was no school dance or graduation ceremony, just a "goodbye" and "good luck" from friends, staff, and teachers.

That summer, my silly Hampton crew would disperse across southeast Michigan. Keith and his family would trade their mini-mansion for a smaller home with an in-ground swimming pool in a safer, more affluent, and predominately white suburb just outside of Detroit. That meant that he would attend Southfield High School in the upcoming school year. Michael, like my cousin Kevin, would attend Cass Technical High School, and Marvin would go on to Mumford High School.

My mother was determined to keep me out of the Detroit Public School system. She wanted me to attend a Catholic high school called Bishop Borgess in Redford, MI.

"Redford?!" I exclaimed incredulously. "How will I get to school every day?"

"Oh, don't worry about that. You just worry about passing the entrance exam."

It was not up for debate. We set out on what seemed like an excursion to Bishop Borgess, a distance I could not imagine going to and from each weekday for four years. Upon our arrival, we were graciously greeted by an administrator and given a tour of Bishop Borgess's impressive campus. Every stereotypically white high school kid I had seen in the movies seemed to have leapt from the screen and was now wandering the halls. For the first time in two years, there was a possibility that I would be in a classroom that was not made entirely of black students. The demographics looked just like the University District's when we first arrived.

I was well aware of the reputation Catholic high schools had for providing an excellent education in a safe environment. But while some of my former teachers at Hampton had occasionally indulged my classroom shenanigans as a welcome alternative to the otherwise violent behavior the other students engaged in so frequently, I feared that my mischievous antics would not be valued by a bunch of priests and nuns.

Moreover, I had become accustomed to going to school with only black people. Everything about my life and my friends' lives in middle school was black: the way we dressed, joked, walked, talked, and fought. The sports we played, the way we interacted with girls, the way we worshiped God, the food we ate, our views toward education: it all had the label of black identity stamped on it. At the time, although I may not have truly comprehended what being black meant I was still *very conscious* of the fact that I was black and not white.

My worries about how many dreaded city buses I would have to ride and the amount of time it would take to get to school every day was only compounded when I noticed the apparent lack of black people at the school.

But I realized that there was no need to worry about attending Bishop Borgess because I was going to very intentionally flunk *the hell* out of that exam.

No sooner had I committed myself to this plan when everything changed. Three gorgeous black girls came walking toward me and my mother. I had an epiphany of sorts. All of a sudden Bishop Borgess looked like it might be *the perfect institution* with which to associate myself.

My mother stopped them. "Are you young ladies here to take the entrance exam?"

One of the girls replied, "Yes, we're taking the exam."

As a teenage boy with raging hormones, I was now very interested in attending Bishop Borgess.

"So, you will be ninth graders. This is my son Andre. He's taking the exam as well."

"Hi," I said.

The girls introduced themselves, and we exchanged some brief pleasantries before they wished me luck and went on their way. One of them reminded me of Lea, and it made me sad to think that I was moving on to high school without her. Because I had not heard anything about Lea in a while, I was left to assume the worst. Then a sudden flash of worry came over me: *would I even pass the entrance exam?*

A few weeks later, my mother and I received a package in the mail from Bishop Borgess. The package included a calendar of events, a student handbook, and an acceptance letter. Bursting with excitement, I skimmed through the handbook. It laid out the high expectations and standards for students attending Bishop Borgess. There was a list of do's and don'ts concerning the dress code. Basically, no suits or ties were required, but no jeans or gym shoes allowed. The package also included a welcome letter signed by Vice Principal Gray that ended with congratulations for being a member of the freshman class of 1989 and of the Bishop Borgess student body of over 2,200 students.

Upon arriving for my first day of school, I found the halls packed with students reacquainting themselves from middle school or the last time they walked the halls of Bishop Borgess. I walked the crowded halls alone, trying to just take it all in when I spotted a six-foot five-inch black kid named Marco Murphy. He had attended Hampton Elementary but left for a different middle school. Although he was not in any of my classes back at Hampton, I was relieved to find at least one person I knew in this new sea of strange faces.

I made my way to my homeroom class before the first bell rang and recognized three kids there that were on the last of the three city buses I had to take to arrive that morning. They were named Tim Young, Reggie Washington, and Jaylin Wilson, and I was delighted to discover that we were all good at making people laugh. What a relief it was that I was able to find a new crew on my first day of school.

From the moment I stepped on the bus to the moment I got off it when we got to school, it was fun and games. I had dreaded these long bus rides for nothing. Our main game was called "capping." Capping, otherwise known as "playing the dozens," was something that I had perfected during my

73

two years of not learning a damn thing at Hampton Middle School. In no time at all, I was recognized as one of the best cappers in the ninth grade.

The first few days of school were pretty good. I joined the freshman football team, the classes weren't too difficult, and there were no dangers or threats to worry about, like there were at my last school.

However, the racial division within the student body was *glaring*. Unlike Hampton Elementary's division of students into those who were studious and those who were not, Bishop Borgess's division was between the black and white kids.

I really noticed this dynamic as a member of the freshman football team. During practice, games, and in the locker room, we were brothers in green—Spartans united against our opponents. But in class and in the hallways, there seemed to be an invisible barrier separating the races similar to the feeling I had whenever I interacted with the Cubic girls. There was no outright animosity, but the baseline of our relationship seemed to start at a polite tolerance.

*

The Pep Rally

A few weeks into my first semester, I overheard a few upperclassmen talking about something called a pep rally. I had no idea what to expect or what a pep rally even was. But as the days passed, I heard more and more excited accounts of it. On the way home one day, I overheard a black upperclassman declare in the unenthusiastic tone of an old man who's seen it all, "It's a bunch of nothing. All of the classes gather in the gym and try to out-cheer each other with stupid chants about school spirit."

The freshman football team did not practice with the junior varsity or varsity teams, so even though the pep rally's purpose was to cheer on the football teams, there was no flow of information concerning what to expect even from the other football teams.

The day of the pep rally came, and the eager anticipation among the upperclassmen was palpable. The freshmen class, especially the minorities, observed them in varying degrees of wonder. Whether fire drill or pep rally, I didn't care; anything was a welcome opportunity to get out of class. It was evident that amongst my peers at Bishop Borgess who shared the same black identity, a pep rally's only merit was the excuse to skip class under the auspices of authority and tradition.

That day, the fourth period was replaced with a directive to report to our homerooms. Upon hearing that, everyone but us clueless freshman was bursting with exhilaration. As we sat in our homeroom class, the vice principal's calm yet stern voice came over the PA.

"Hello, Bishop Borgess students and staff." There was a pause. His next words were like bullets out of an automatic rifle: "Are. You. Ready. For. The. Pep. Rally?!"

The classrooms around ours exploded with cheers. When he asked for quiet, you could hear a pin drop. Clearly, being the harbinger of the pep rally imbued him with a high level of authority.

The vice principal went on to bark over the PA about school history, school pride, school spirit, and how, as students of Bishop Borgess, we had to support our sports teams.

He passionately went on about school rivalries and how it was so important that Borgess football finally beat Brother Rice Catholic High School and Catholic Central High School.

However, my black identity would not allow me to celebrate this institution's history. It was likely filled with racists and racism. Those who shared this black identity would participate in school activities like pep rallies with feelings ranging from indifference to animosity, while our white counterparts, who were not responsible for past sins at Bishop Borgess, were left to look upon us like, "Well it wasn't my fault and it's not my problem."

Then, as if he were a general commanding his best brigade to advance upon an enemy, he barked, "Seniors, report to the gym."

The order cast a spell on the seniors, compelling them to run to the gym like screeching maniacs. He called the juniors next in the same manner, who tried to out-scream the seniors as they took to the halls. Then he called upon the sophomores, and they tried to out-scream the juniors and the seniors.

The vice principal took an extended pause as he waited until the halls cleared. Finally, he asked the freshman class to report to the gym. As we moved through the halls, some of my classmates tried to imitate our predecessors, but it was obviously a half-hearted attempt to mimic an activity they did not truly understand.

My classroom was the first of the freshmen to arrive at the entrance to the gym. We were not allowed to enter, as it was customary that the entire freshman class is announced and enter together. As we waited, we could hear rock music playing over the PA system, and I could see cheerleaders leading the crowd in chants. The seniors sat together in chairs at the far end of the gym floor, the juniors were next to them closer towards the entrance, and the sophomores sat in bleachers facing the juniors. This meant that we would have to march in front of the entire student body to get to our seats, which were facing the seniors. Once we were all gathered in the hall outside the gym, we were announced to the rest of the student body of Bishop Borgess as the class of 1989 and lead into the fray.

We were greeted with chants of "fresh meat!" and little playful boos and hisses. The loudest hecklers were the sophomores; it was their turn to give us what they got the year before. As we took our seats, two things became clear: the class of '89 was the largest class, and it had the highest percentage of black students.

After we were seated, various teachers and coaches followed the vice principal's lead and started talking about school spirit over the gym's PA system. One teacher took the microphone and proclaimed, "Now it's time to see who has the most school spirit. We'll start with the seniors!"

The seniors responded by chanting Queen's iconic "We Will, We Will Rock You!" As they did, they pointed emphatically at the rest of the student body. After a few rounds of this from the seniors, the teacher asked to hear from the juniors, who followed suit with another Queen classic, "Another One

Bites the Dust." Then it was the sophomores' turn to do the same, and they sang an awful rendition of Survivor's "Eye of the Tiger."

All the upper classes were so prepared, I was starting to wonder if I had not gotten the memo. But as I looked up and down the rows, it was apparent that no one in the class of 1989 got the memo. We did not have a chant. When the teacher finally got around to calling on the freshmen, we simply sat there. Our stupefied silence was the biggest spectacle of the pep rally, and we sulked in embarrassment. The rest of the student body smelled blood and rained down boos, jeers, and laughter upon us.

"We'll do this again, and the next round we'll see what type of school spirit the class of '89 comes up with," the teacher interrupted. Like many who shared my black identity, I didn't like or listen to rock music. I was at a loss for a rock song to sing. As the seniors resumed their "We Will Rock You" routine, I turned to my friend Reggie and joked, "We should do 'La Di Da Di.'"

"La Di Da Di" was a rap song by Doug E. Fresh, who was very popular among black youth. I had suggested the song in jest. At the time, many adults—black or white, but especially white Catholic priests and nuns— frowned upon rap music. Reggie passed the idea over to Tim, and he loved it. With a bit of defiance in our voice, the three of us started in.

"*La Di Da Di we like to party, we don't cause trouble, we don't bother nobody. We're just the class that's on the mic, and when we rock up on the mic, we rock the mic right!*"

It instantly caught on, and other students around us started singing: "*La Di Da Di we like to party, we don't cause trouble, we don't bother nobody. We're just the class that's on the mic, and when we rock up on the mic, we rock the mic right!*"

As the juniors began their chant, "La Di Da Di" had spread like fire among the class of '89, and we were ready to let the other classes have it. Every kid in school that identified with the black identity knew that rap song. A lot of the white kids did not know the song or even listen to rap music for that matter, but "La Di Da Di" was so catchy and easy to recite that even white kids in the class of '89 adopted it willingly. When it was our turn to do our thing, the freshmen hit Bishop Borgess High School with "La Di Da Di" as the other classes, faculty, and staff listened in astonishment.

*

The class of '89 had brought rap and everything it stood for to a pep rally at a Catholic high school. When we arrived at Bishop Borgess, rap was considered by many in the administration and student body as an unwelcome aspect of our black identity. At times, aspects of our identity seemed to be in direct contradiction with the status quo at Bishop Borgess. That contradiction made life at Bishop Borgess uncomfortable at times. In fact, by the end of the first semester, rapping in the halls was banned. It was easy for black students to consider that decision by the white administration as one based on racism, whether it was or not one could only speculate. But we didn't speculate—we *accused.*

In those days, hip-hop was still in its infancy, and most people over thirty didn't understand the appeal of MCs rapping and DJs scratching. The white students, faculty, and staff, as well as the community at large, were not extremely fond of rap music's neighborhood-disturbing base and often-offensive lyrics. But black kids like us in the inner cities had created rap, so it was easy for us to interpret the dislike for rap by whites as another piece of circumstantial evidence that whites just didn't like blacks.

Although my friends and I didn't make much of an effort to be friends with the white kids either, there were exceptions. The white kids who enjoyed rap, participated in certain athletics, and engaged in bad social behavior were welcomed into black circles as people who appreciated the black identity.

Conversely, black kids who were studious were rejected by their black peers as not being *black enough.*

Despite not studying, I finished my first year of high school with average grades. I had made plenty of friends, and when the last bell of the semester rang to welcome in summer vacation, I looked forward to returning in the fall.

*

The Ring

The summer between the ninth and tenth grades came with the now-normal exodus of new residents, both white and black, from the neighborhood. What was most significant for me, though, was that Juan, Tracy, and Lacy had all moved out of the neighborhood. Juan's parents bought a new home, while

Tracy and Lacy felt it was time to leave the nest and get their own place. Although the Cubics still remained, Tim and I hardly ever saw each other, and the Cubic sisters seemed to have just disappeared.

Tenth grade began with an unexpected turn of events at Bishop Borgess. Though the incoming freshman class was noticeably smaller than the class of '89, the percentage of black students was noticeably higher than all of the previous classes. Furthermore, Bishop Borgess's student population and the class of 1989 itself was practically halved. The rumor was that a significant portion of the school's population had chosen to go to a Catholic school in Detroit that had more of a black presence, or otherwise switched to a Catholic school further away from Detroit with less of a black presence.

The already chasmic racial divide at Bishop Borgess just kept getting wider. But no one, certainly not I, seemed to really care. Honestly, I never felt like the faculty and staff thought that black kids were intellectually inferior. In fact, the class of 89 would eventually produce co-valedictorians: one black and one white. That racial divide was just a way of life with no real logic or consequences. That is, until one seemingly ordinary day in the hallway between classes.

While I was talking to my locker neighbor Marcus and shifting through the contents of my locker, our friend Jaylin approached us. We were all members of the class of 89.

Jaylin turned to me and asked, "Do you want this? I just found it on the floor." He was holding out a ring in the palm of his hand.

"Nah, man that's too small for my finger," I said. "And isn't that a girl's ring anyway?"

Jaylin turned to Marcus. "How about you?"

"Nah, that is definitely a chick's ring. No thanks."

At that point, we all went to our separate classes and thought nothing more about the ring. Later that day, I was sitting in English class when we heard a calm and sweet-sounding female voice interrupt our lesson over the PA system: "Will the following students please report to Vice Principal Gray's office immediately: Marcus Jenkins and Andre Davis."

Marcus and I arrived at the vice principal's office at the same time. We had no idea why we were there until we saw Jaylin. *The ring!* Marcus was called into Mr. Gray's office first. Mr. Gray then told me to sit down on the opposite side of the room from Jaylin and to keep my mouth shut. His assistant nodded her head to assure him that she was ready to enforce his decree.

Though we couldn't speak with each other, I attempted to convey my confusion with my eyes. His eyes replied, "Man, this is some bullshit," while he pointed to his finger.

Just as I suspected, it was about that stupid ring. Marcus was in the vice principal's office for about ten minutes. When he came out, his eyes were wide with disbelief. Mr. Gray followed him out and told him to have a seat. Then I was called into the vice principal's office.

With an unforgiving look, he said, "Jaylin tells me that he asked you to take a ring off his hands that he found in the hall. Is that correct?"

"Yes, that is correct," I responded. I was unable to hold back a nervous smile.

Then, in his usual matter of fact tone, he told me that I was being suspended from school for three days for failing to return the ring.

"The school handbook clearly states that if you find an item that doesn't belong to you, the item must be brought to the vice principal's office."

I was shocked. I pleaded, "I did not find the ring. Jaylin found the ring. The ring is worthless. It's a toy ring. I don't think it has any value whatsoever."

Mr. Gray narrowed his eyes. "That is where you are wrong. This is why the rule is in the handbook. That ring is a family heirloom of Jessica Stevens. Do you know her?"

"No."

"She is a member of your class."

"Sorry, but I do not know her."

"Well, she spotted Jaylin with the ring, and when she asked him for it back, he said it was not hers, but his. More importantly, the way he said it made her feel threatened. That's why she came to me."

"Threatened?" This was absurd. I shook my head. "Jaylin is five-foot three and one hundred pounds."

"Well, Jessica is four-foot eight and eighty-five pounds."

"But what does that have to do with me? I didn't even find the ring. I never even touched it. Jaylin asked me if I wanted the ring and I said, no."

"According to the handbook, every student at this school has the responsibility to turn in any lost items to my office."

Karma and racism: that was all I could think of at that moment. When I was in middle school, I was guilty of feeling up a black girl. But, I had lied about what really happened and got away with it because of my reputation as a good student. This time, I was charged with not turning in a ring that my black friend Jaylin had found, which unbeknownst to me belonged to a white girl. Even though I told the truth about it, I got punished anyway because of my reputation as a black student.

I was certain that if Marcus and I were white, the application of the student handbook law would not have been as severe and neither one of us would have been suspended. I went home that night and angrily told my mother and Lee, who was now my stepfather, that I had been suspended from school. I was expecting them to be outraged.

"So tell me again why you were excluded?" my stepfather asked.

"Because my black friend, Jaylin, found this white girl's ring in the hall, and when he asked Marcus and I if one of us wanted the ring we both said, no. That is why we got suspended from school."

With a look of slight confusion, my mother asked again, "Why are you being suspended?"

"I'm being suspended because I did not force my black friend, Jaylin, to return a white girl's worthless-looking ring to the vice principal's office. Vice Principal Gray said I had a duty to tell Jaylin to return the ring. Otherwise, I should have returned the ring to his office myself. He said that, according to the student handbook, if a student finds something on school property that does not belong to said student, then that student must turn in the item to the vice principal's office."

I expected her to contact Mr. Gray and tell him that he was wrong for excluding me. Instead, I was punished and told that I had to learn how to follow the rules in this world.

*

Viewed as birds of a feather

I truly believed that our race weighed heavily in Mr. Gray's decision to exclude not only Jaylin but all three of us. Jaylin had been in hot water before, and his decisions, actions, and misplaced priorities had earned him a reputation for being a troublemaker. Marcus and I, on the other hand, had never been in trouble. We merely happened to be Jaylin's friends who shared his black identity. Feeling unwelcome at school from time to time allowed me to rationalize my disdain for its traditional culture of academic rigor.

Upon our return from our forced vacation, we were met with an overwhelming response that Mr. Gray was a racist asshole that wanted to rid Bishop Borgess of every black student that he could.

While that may have been true in part, the vice principal surely saw the situation from a broader perspective. The fact was that Bishop Borgess had begun to rapidly lose its reputation for academic excellence. Consequently, school administrators were seeing an exodus of coveted students who actually came to school to get an education.

To stop the swiftly-moving outward flow of students, school administrators were attempting to purge the school of students who were obviously not there to learn. Before being excluded, I had never met Mr. Gray. There was no evidence to tell him that I was a troublemaker. But my association with Jaylin and my 2.5 GPA certainly did not contradict his assumptions.

The problem was that the black identity did not value academic rigor. Although unfair, it was easy for Mr. Gray to conclude that three black students that he did not know personally were not at Borgess with academics as a priority. Many of my black peers and I went to Bishop Borgess primarily for safety, rather than to obtain skills to help us compete in America's free market. Many of us had lost faith in the promise of a good education to provide upward social mobility.

In the meantime, the school had to pay its bills. So, students who did not value education but whose parents could afford the tuition at Bishop Borgess, kept on enrolling. Meanwhile, those students who were attending Bishop Borgess for an incredible education that would one day make them competitive members of a free market society were being disturbed in class and threatened in the halls by students like Jaylin.

*

Drug dealers and Pigeons

Outside of school, I was dealing with a rapidly changing reality in the black community. The Cool was dead, and The Thug had entirely replaced it. The Thug wasn't as readily accepted amongst black people as The Cool had been. However, it wasn't wholeheartedly rejected either.

The Thug and his drug money seemed to be tolerated in part because of the perceived lack of opportunities in mainstream America for black youth. As a result, the stigma associated with being a drug dealer had been minimized, and a black drug dealer's road to quick money was one with few hurdles. In fact, even if kids weren't selling drugs they found little resistance in *appearing to be* selling drugs.

One sunny day, I rode my bike over to my cousin Kevin's house and saw him washing a brand-new sports car. It was not just any sports car—it was a customized Mustang 5.0 GT. Black-on-black with a ground effect kit, custom rims, and T-tops. Something no child would be expected to own. But that everyone one would expect a drug dealer to own. I almost jumped right out of my shoes.

"Whose is this?"

"Mine," he replied with a surprising degree of nonchalance.

"How did you get this? Your mom bought it?"

"Yup, I got it for my birthday."

"When was your birthday?"

"It's a few weeks from now."

87

I wondered to myself why he had received a birthday present weeks ahead of time but didn't ask. It seemed like a trivial question. Instead, I helped him finish washing the car and started a new era in my life.

This new era began with a twenty-minute ride around the neighborhood. It lasted only twenty minutes because unlicensed Kevin had to illegally drive himself to driver's training class. During that ride, we were the subject of a lot of fanfare, attracting attention like a wardrobe malfunction on a busty woman. From that day forward, whenever we drove around in Kevin's car, we instantly became the object of any girl's desire and every guy's envy. I felt like Superman.

Instead of playing Atari, my time with Kevin was now spent cruising the streets of Detroit and collecting phone numbers from girls, young ladies, and *women*. We would go to the mall and come out with phone numbers left on the windshield like parking tickets. It never seemed to matter how old we were, how we looked, or if we were teenage criminals—possession of *that car* met or exceeded the standards of many females in Detroit.

Drug dealers in Detroit were becoming as common as pigeons and they were raising the bar on showing affection to girls. Easy drug money fed the natural desire to want to impress girls, and gift giving skyrocketed to ridiculous levels. Being able to write poetry, articulate some great ambition, or having a great intellect no longer got a guy very far with the ladies. As I was once told by a girl, I was pursuing: "I can walk by myself. You need to get a car." At the time, I wasn't old enough for a driver's license.

Girls who were attracted to drug dealers for the expensive gifts they gave became known as Sack-Chasers. Unlike the valuables they craved, they were often viewed as cheap commodities easily purchased for quick consumption. Of course, not all girls in Detroit were Sack-Chasers. But their existence had what you could call a trickle-down effect on the rest of the female population. Likewise, not all guys in Detroit sold drugs, but the abundance of dealers had a trickle-down effect as well. It became very apparent that a guy could become the apple of a girl's eye if he had drug money. Or, as it was in my cousin's case, "appeared" to have drug money.

Before you knew it, tons of Detroit's youth started to look, dress, and act like drug dealers. This trend only added to the affection for criminal and deviant behavior, as well as reinforcing its attachment to the black identity.

Compared to the black identity responsible for the black's gains in legal equality and the black identity before and after emancipation that revered education, the modern black identity's low social standards and low scholastic expectations were bewildering.

Although blacks were now equal before the law, the reality was that social equality remained a dream. This feeling of inequality that Tracy and Lacy warned me about, and that my peers and I were feeling, wasn't racial inequality it was social inequality.

Social Equality

"The wisest among my race understand that the agitation of questions of social equality is the extremest folly and that progress and the privileges that would come to us must be the result of severe pain and constant struggle rather than of artificial forcing. No race that has anything to contribute to the markets of the world is long in any degree ostracized. It is important and right that all privileges of the law be ours but it is vastly more important that we be prepared for the exercises of these privileges. The opportunity to earn a dollar in a factory just now is worth infinitely more than the opportunity to spend a dollar in an opera house."

--Booker T. Washington speech at the Atlanta Exposition 1895

Social equality is a just level of value that a society sees in one of its members relative to another member. For example, a citizen with the stigma of a felony is not considered socially equal to a law-abiding citizen. Racism, as Tracy and Lacy understood it, is a belief that a person is superior to another, solely due to genetics, and that this superiority complex was what caused whites to discriminate against them as blacks.

Of course, there are racists in American society. However, no Ku Klux Klansmen were preventing my Hampton Middle School crew from studying math, nor were there Klansmen selling drugs on the corners or compelling us to do same. These were all self-inflicted wounds.

The distinction between social inequality and racial inequality is important for a very simple reason. Your race is fixed and objective—but social equality is adjustable and subjective. In other words, you can't choose how you are born, but you can choose how you live.

Young people in Detroit's neighborhoods were embracing standards so low that respect was garnered from their ability to purchase or steal expensive gym shoes or handbags and not from intellectual or economic achievements.

Our black identity, for the most part, admired short-term consumption rather than long-term production. We believed that social inequality was fixed, like a person's race, and we let that belief erode our faith in a better life through academic achievement, good social values, and positive social behavior.

Drug dealers, pro-athletes, and pimps became our role models. Moreover, we put a monetary minimum on success. What mattered was being able to flaunt the material symbols of wealth rather than obtaining the skills that would allow for the creation of our own personal wealth.

Along with the drugs on the streets and the bullets flying through the air, Detroit's atmosphere was thick with a weaponized drug dealer mentality that welcomed hostility over the most trivial of things. Contrary to my life in the projects where people addressed each other with dignity and respect, now you couldn't make eye contact with strangers without being challenged to a fight. We were in a constant state of tension and everyone's guard was up.

In spite of the new black identity's narrative of victimization and hopelessness, numerous black people not only still valued education but they also kept their faith in education. There *were* black kids who had long-term

91

goals—don't get me wrong. There were still black parents aiming to pass their strong work ethic onto their kids. There were also young black adults who aspired to live in safer neighborhoods and raise their own families. The black people who believed in the traditional, tried-and-true kinds of values that lead to one achieving success in a free market society were not going extinct. They were just going to suburbia.

*

College?

By the time I made it to eleventh grade, I had fallen in love with the idea of going to college. Seemingly overnight, I went from not even thinking about life after high school to wanting nothing more than to receive an acceptance letter. This was all thanks to *The Cosby Show* and its highly anticipated spin-off *A Different World*.

A Different World was about black students at a historically black college. Its cast, which encompassed faculty, staff, and students, was nearly all black. It only took a few episodes to completely sell me on the idea of going to college. It reminded me of a better version of Hampton Middle School: a place where I'd be surrounded by black people without a single Mr. Gray to be found.

The truth was that I just wanted to go to college to have fun. There was a real disconnect, for me, between going to college and going to college to accomplish something as difficult as becoming a physician, like the Cosby Show's Dr. Huxtable.

Some kids had decided to go to college while they were still in elementary school, and their entire academic lives were carefully organized and meticulously planned towards this goal. My belated desire to attend college, suddenly discovered in my penultimate year of high school, put me roughly a decade behind these students. In comparison, I was overwhelmingly underprepared. Still, it was better late than never.

But, before I could even be considered for admittance to a college, I had to take a national scholastic aptitude exam. It was crucial that I do well on this if I were to get into a good college. So, in the autumn of eleventh grade, I endeavored to take something that felt less like a test and more like a scholastic marathon. While I had only studied for a few weeks, I was competing against other students who had been preparing for years. With the odds stacked highly against me, I did my best and left it in God's hands.

Even if I did well on the test, I knew that I would need to get my GPA up. My mother, elated that I had this renewed interest in learning, presented me with a new source of motivation: if I managed to make the honor roll that term, she promised to buy me my friend Samuel's Honda Elite 150cc scooter, provided that it was still available.

Though I was ill-prepared to turn my idea of going to college into reality, the promise of finding that sleek scooter in the driveway made me pretty damn motivated to give it my best shot. I happily agreed to her terms. After all, making the honor roll would not only get me a scooter, it would also help me get into college. Two birds, one stone.

From then on, I was going to school with purpose. I started taking my books home and paying attention in class. Instead of using class time to show off my comedy skills, I found myself offering answers to the teacher's questions. For the first time since the sixth grade, I took a genuine interest in my grades. I went back to being one of the smart students. I made the honor roll that semester and brought home straight A's the next semester too. My mother was a woman of her word. In addition to earning myself a real shot at a college acceptance, I'd bought my freedom in the form of a Honda Elite 150 scooter just in time for summer vacation.

*

Historically Black College Tour

Coinciding with my new love for academia, my friend Steve from the football team offered me the opportunity to accompany him and his parents on a spontaneous, makeshift tour of a few historically black colleges. It would be within the first few weeks of summer vacation, and the tour would include Hampton University in Hampton Virginia, Howard University in Washington, D.C., as well as North Carolina A&T University, and North Carolina Central University in Greensboro and Durham respectively. The duration of the tour would be seven days and it would cost my parents and me absolutely nothing. How could I refuse?

On each campus, Steve and I talked to as many guys and girls as we possibly could to get a sense of what it was like to attend college there. Talking to actual college students about student life only made my desire to attend college that much stronger. The fantasy was now becoming a tangible reality.

Second only to the abundance of freedom that I would gain from leaving the nest was the prospect of living amongst a population of people who had not been infected by the Sack-Chaser virus. No one on any of the campuses had even heard the term before.

We were in heaven. College life appeared to be just like it was on TV. Our interactions with the other male students were always welcoming and encouraging. Our interactions with the females on campus were even better, peppered with inquiries about where we were from and which major were we thinking about declaring.

After talking to countless administrators and students at four incredible historically black colleges, our tour came to an end. Though Steve and I were sad to leave, we were extremely excited about the possibility of going to a historically black college the next year. I returned home and jumped on my scooter like Paul Revere leaping atop his horse. Instead of telling everyone someone was coming, I proudly declared that I was leaving.

*

Black life

On the first day of my final year of high school, Steve picked me up in a brand-new Honda Civic. It had tinted windows, a rag top, and shiny chrome rims. We were Catholic school students who looked like successful drug dealers.

95

We expected the student population to have shrunk a little bit as it had every year. But we were shocked and disappointed to discover that the entire student body had been reduced to a paltry group smaller than the original class of 1989. Moreover, the makeup of the student body had reversed. It was now approximately seventy percent black, twenty percent white, and ten percent other races. White flight was over. The whites had flown.

As I crept toward adulthood, my world was getting smaller and smaller. Regardless, I interpreted my school's metamorphosis into one with a predominantly black student body to be a blessing. By the twelfth grade, I wanted nothing to do with anything or anyone that wasn't black. I felt that as long as I cocooned myself inside of black America, I would be free from the ills of a racist society that existed beyond its boundaries. That feeling persisted even though I knew, deep inside, that I was more likely to be killed by another young black male than any white male outside of my black cocoon. But it didn't matter. I felt most secure when I was interacting with other black people.

The Cosby Show and *A Different World* were so appealing to me because they provided a glimpse into a future after high school that was an expanded version of the black cocoon that I did not want to leave.

From my black cocoon, I was looking out into another world where whites and people of other races competed at an extremely high level academically, were enrolled in Ivy League schools and huge state universities, and went on to compete in America's free marketplace with all the advantages that degrees from those institutions would afford.

96

They were the people who wrote books about butterflies and patented such things as different kinds of adhesives. They went to national dog shows, explored the oceans and space alike, created life-extending drugs, and developed computer programs. In that world they climbed mountains, traveled to remote nations, and learned foreign languages. Yet people with my black identity seemed to always be ready on the outside of that world to entertain them with a beautiful song, an amazing dance, or an incredible athletic feat. My black identity did not allow me to see myself—or any black person I would have considered *real,* living in that world.

*

The Sack Chasers' Ball

Twelfth grade flew by without a hitch. Though my results from the standard aptitude test were by no means stellar, when combined with my new GPA, I hoped it would be enough to get me into one of the four colleges that I had visited.

With that in mind, everything I did and every decision I made was influenced by the possibility of attending college in the fall of 1989. I continued to get excellent grades and decided to get a job, not really to help pay for tuition and books, but for the fresh clothes I would need to wear on campus.

I applied to be a cashier on the night shift at a neighborhood diner called Ram's Horn 24-Hour Family Restaurant. I had been there a few times to eat lunch or an early dinner and noticed that most of the patrons were white and qualified for senior citizen discounts. There was never a shortage of retired auto workers. My skills, however lacking they were, and my smile got me hired on the spot.

In addition to manning the cash register, I was to greet and seat customers as well. My hours were from 11 PM to 7 AM on Fridays and Saturdays. I looked forward to the night shift because I envisioned getting paid while studying in an empty restaurant. However, on the night I started, the manager informed me that the place was actually pretty lively after 2 AM.

"After the clubs close everyone in Detroit comes here for the after party," he said.

I hadn't heard of any clubs nearby so, I assumed that the manager was exaggerating to make sure I didn't slack off.

I arrived early on my first day to get acquainted with the cash register and staff. From 9 PM until 1 AM, things were so slow that I found myself drinking several cups of coffee to stay awake. In fact, the place was entirely empty from 11 PM to half past midnight.

Pam, a seasoned waitress, warned me to be careful of drinking so much coffee, lest I'd be unable to sleep when I finally got home. She also reminded me that there would soon be plenty of activity to keep me going.

Pam was a black lady in her forties. She was voluptuous with a beautiful face. She had an air of professionalism and dignity that made her stand head and shoulders above the other waitresses. Her professionalism told me to take what she said seriously.

As promised, at 2 AM, I was dealing with impatient customers waiting in a line that wrapped around the front of the restaurant's large bay windows. By 2:30 AM, the restaurant was jam-packed. The wait time to be seated reached sixty minutes. Ram's Horn had totally transformed from a diner serving mostly retired white auto workers to an after-hours joint serving Detroit's best-dressed drug dealers and their Sack-Chasers.

The customers looked as if they were going to an awards show. Every woman was dressed to impress; the cut of their dresses or the fit of their jeans conveyed only bad intentions. Their hairstyles were so impressively crafted that I couldn't help but imagine a team of architects and contractors spending hours putting it together. All of a sudden, I was the host at the Sack-Chasers' Ball.

The guys dressed as if they had just stepped off the front page of *Drug Dealer Lifestyle Weekly*. Every guy ordering a breakfast special wore gold chains and expensive, non-prescription glasses. Guys for whom buying expensive clothes off the rack wasn't enough wore custom-made attire: denim jackets with airbrushed portraits of themselves outlined in rhinestone that in some cases cost thousands of dollars. Until then, I never knew alligator shoes could come in pink, yellow, lime green, sky blue, and turquoise, all on the same shoe.

The parking lot looked like a car show. There were new, custom-painted Mercedes, BMWs, and Jaguars, as well as pristine classic cars and trucks. Every girl there was infected with the Sack-Chaser virus, and every guy there, except the restaurant staff, had what she needed.

99

My plan to use the restaurant as a nighttime library went up in smoke. The crowd would get rowdy at times. But between the constant presence of plainclothes cops and Pam walking the aisles of the restaurant demanding respect from all the thugs, things typically stayed calm. The occasional rowdiness was tolerated because the drug dealers would order everything on the menu and tipped us very well. They threw their easy money around as though it were a sin to keep it. I would get tips of $15 on a $5 bill.

On Mondays, I would report what I experienced at Ram's Horn to my friends at school. Along with the weekly car and fashion report always came a disheartening story about thugs, looking like Star War's Jabba the Hutt with a Jheri curl dating the prettiest girls I had ever seen. It was just plain criminal.

*

Out of Detroit and into Adulthood

One day, a letter arrived from North Carolina Central University. As I held the unopened envelope in my hands, I felt all of my hopes and dreams riding on whatever was inside and nervously went about opening it as if I were defusing a bomb. It turned out to be my acceptance letter. I had gone from being oblivious to the possibility of going college, to getting onto the honor roll at Bishop Borgess, to ultimately being accepted at NCCU—all within about a year's time.

When high school graduation arrived, family and friends flocked to congratulate me and praise my parents for doing such a great job raising me. I had lived up to my parents' expectations, but to many in Detroit's black

100

community, I had exceeded expectations simply by arriving at adulthood all in one piece.

Part II

Chapter 6

University Life

On an early August morning in 1989, I said goodbye to my parents and headed to North Carolina Central University with my friends, Steve and Marco. The boys from Borgess were headed to NCCU.

A week before classes began, we arrived on campus for freshman orientation. The first thing we did was go to the Housing Department to obtain keys to our dorm rooms. Steve and I would be roommates in Chidley Hall, and Marco would be rooming with a guy named David from Wilmington, NC on the floor above us. Chidley Hall was the lone male dorm on campus. Much to our delight, we discovered that there were five full dorms of girls. There was also a co-ed dorm on campus, but it was reserved exclusively for honors students.

It didn't hit me how much freedom I would have as a college student until that first night on campus. As the sun started to set, I realized that I had not phoned my family yet. After calling them to let them know I was okay, I was hit with the strange realization that I would not have to phone again unless there was a school-related issue to discuss. I did not have to tell them where I was going, when I was going to bed, who I was hanging out with, or what I was doing in general. So, I did what all sheltered children do the moment they are freed: I lost my damn mind and enjoyed every minute of it.

That very night, Steve, Marco, and I made a spontaneous trip to the grocery store. Steve dared me to see if I could buy us one 40-ounce bottle of Colt 45 malt liquor. Whether one bottle or three, I figured it was all the same. So, I walked over to the counter and handed the cashier three 40-ounce bottles of beer and some money. In return, I received an indifferent glance, some change, and a bag with three 40-ounce bottles of beer.

I walked back to the car holding what would become the driving force of my freshman year at NCCU. I had never taken a sip of beer before illegally purchasing it that night. All three of us opened our bottles, toasted to our new life, and proceeded to get drunk. In that wasted state, we decided to introduce ourselves to the students hanging out on campus that night. Marco's roommate, David, suggested that we go to a spot near the girls' dorms called the Quad. He told us that is where everyone hangs out at night. We stammered and stumbled our way over to the Quad and rumor has it that we had a *great time.*

The next day, I felt absolutely awful, but despite our raging hangovers, the four of us managed to get ourselves together and trudge to stand in line after line to register for classes and financial aid. As we hung around the registration lobby, a few of our schoolmates happily shed some light on the hazy events of the night before.

Apparently, I had been very talkative and friendly, walking around introducing myself to every girl on campus and taking pictures with them. I even tried hitting on a girl whose friend had just rejected my stumbling advances thirty-seconds prior. Luckily, Steve had been still-sober enough to apologize on my behalf and had assured them that I was harmless. We had played the role of Detroit's most silly ambassadors, clothed head to toe in Detroit Tigers and Pistons gear, drunk but friendly. That night, we became known as the boys from Detroit.

*

. . . And now, the amazing Negro

It was not long before we heard of another guy from Detroit who attended NCCU the year before who was well known amongst the student body. From how people spoke about him, he seemed like a legend. Accounts of his exploits varied, and we couldn't tell if he was a great guy or a complete asshole.

One day as we stood in line for lunch at the cafeteria, we heard a loud, high-pitched voice from somewhere behind us. It had the smooth cadence of a pimp's smooth croon in some Blaxploitation film.

"Yo, excuse me! Excuse me! Y'all from Detroit, right?" Suddenly, we realized the slim, dark-skinned young man with big, expressive eyes under long eyelashes was calling for us. "I'm Cicero!"

Talking as if we were the only people in the cafeteria, he made his approach. I observed that he was just a hair shorter than me at five feet nine inches.

Speaking at a slight yell he said "Yo, I heard that there were three hard-ass brothers from The D on campus. I've been looking for Y'all. You staying in Chidley, right?"

"Yeah," we replied in unison. I could not help but wonder where he'd gotten the idea that we were "hard."

"Yeah, I stayed there my freshman year, too. I think you have to. I'm a sophomore now, and I live in the honors dorm."

At this point, he had cut right into the line. As we proceeded to grab our food and sit down, Cicero invited himself along. He went on to tell us about how many girls would be sneaking through our dorm window every night. He also told us about his old roommate, Dee, from Harlem. It was immediately obvious that the guy had the gift of gab. His chatter was somewhat fantastic but mostly uncontroversial. Then, he started to elaborate on the New Yorkers.

"The New Yorkers on campus think that they are God's gift to the world. Now we can stand up to those scrubs."

I looked at him in total bewilderment. How had this already turned into a turf war?

"I keep telling them, 'y'all might be the shit on campus now, but that's because I'm the only Detroiter at this school. If I had just one more homie here from The D, we would *run* this campus," he proclaimed.

Never mind the fact that we had just met him a few minutes ago—he spoke as if we had already assured him that we had his back.

We all looked at Cicero in wonder. What was he talking about? As we all left the cafeteria, Cicero's mouth continued to run nonstop. His monologue was interrupted only by his frequent greetings to students we passed. He was like a local politician the night before an election in a neighborhood of constituents.

From new freshmen to seniors, he'd greet guys and girls alike with a cheerful "What's up shorty?"

The responses varied from a happy "Hey, Cicero!" to an indifferent acknowledgment of "Hello…Cicero."

A few disgruntled male voices were asking, "Where's my money, Cicero?"

One day after classes, Cicero and Marco met up with Steve and me in our room. In tow was a guy with a very light complexion and green eyes. It was Dee from Harlem, Cicero's old roommate. "So, these are your boys from Detroit," he said. He seemed welcoming but skeptical, though we couldn't tell if the skepticism was directed at Cicero or at us.

Dee Boogie, as we came to call him, had a refreshing 70s super-coolness about him. Dee had a very calm nature that made Cicero seem as though he was on speed. Every story Cicero told was on the edge of believability, whereas Dee spoke as if he were constantly under oath. It became clear that they had a great deal of love for each other, though Dee was absolutely the big brother trying to keep his little brother out of trouble.

We were all instant friends. Cicero and Dee proceeded to fill us in on the goings-on of campus life. They gave us the lowdown on parties and dorms and informed us of the groups and social order of NCCU, including the black locals that students derisively called "Durmites."

106

During those first few days, Cicero, with the pride and enthusiasm of a boxing promoter, took us under his wing and introduced us to virtually everyone on campus. I absolutely loved it. Good or bad, we had instant clout. And with our newfound clout, we noticed that our interactions with random girls on campus seemed to lead to great conversations about what we were interested in studying or what we were planning on doing that weekend.

Although Steve had a car, we understood right away that a car or a wad of cash was not necessary to get and keep a girl's attention. Although our style of dress and Steve's car could have been construed as an attempt to imitate the average drug dealer back in Detroit, the girls on campus were not aware of this association. However, Cicero was aware of it, and he made the most out of it.

"Yo, shorty. These are my boys from Detroit and they are hard as hell!" he'd loudly and proudly proclaim to any girl he presented us to.

After a few of these kinds of introductions, I finally asked in a tone that suggested that I should know but had forgotten, "Why are you telling these people we are hard?"

"Don't worry," he responded joyfully, "We are going to run this campus!"

When Cicero was not in our presence, we'd find ourselves asking one another if we believed certain stories told by Cicero to be true. Did his father own Harbor Enterprises? Had he had sex with all those girls? We sought the counsel of Dee Boogie. True to form, Dee gave it to us straight.

"Look, more than half of the things Cicero tells you are lies. The reason everyone in Chidley Hall knows him is because he owes them all money. The reason every girl on campus knows him is because he has tried to hit on all of them. I mean, don't get me wrong. I love Cicero like a brother. But don't lend him money, and don't believe his bullshit. Just do what I do and have fun with him at arm's length."

Then, with his left eyebrow slightly raised, Dee asked a question he seemed to already know the answer to: "Is Cicero really from Detroit, or some prissy, white suburb?"

The question virtually answered itself, but I countered with a question, "Why don't you think he is from Detroit?"

"Since the end of last semester and especially since you brothers arrived, he has been trying to act like something he wasn't. When I first met him, he was an honors student and he had a steady girlfriend that he talked to every day at Bennett College."

"Bennett College?" We all asked simultaneously.

"Oh, it is a women's only historically black college near North Carolina A&T." He said with a grin.

The grin turned into a frown as he got back to the subject at hand. "Yeah. Now, since you guys arrived, he is trying to act all hard, claiming to run the campus, and talking like a pimp."

Steve had heard enough. He said with a contemptuous growl, "He ain't from Detroit. You know all those times he gets street intersections and

108

landmarks wrong? If he really grew up in Detroit, there's no way he would get those things wrong."

Addressing Dee now he continued, "Cicero said he grew up on Grand Lake Avenue and 6 Mile Road, but there is no Grand Lake Avenue. It's called Grand River Avenue. Nobody from Detroit would utter such nonsense like Grand Lake Avenue."

Steve, Marco, and I looked at each other before bursting into a fit of laughter. We all wondered the same thing: Why is he lying?

*

The Southern Belle vs. The Sack-Chaser

A few days later, as we watched TV in our room, Cicero walked right in without knocking and announced that we had to go to Bennett College that night. Steve asked why and Cicero explained that he had to see his girlfriend. Steve was understandably opposed to the excursion, being that it was Thursday night and Bennett College was about an hour away. It was his first attempt at refusing a request from Cicero. But, as we would all come to learn, if Cicero asked for something, he sure as hell got it.

After some ineffectual resistance, the boys from Borgess found ourselves driving off to Bennett College on a school night at his behest.

Once we arrived and found parking, we just followed Cicero's lead. He went to the girl at the front desk of his girlfriend's dorm and asked for her to be called down to the lobby. Although Cicero had claimed all during the drive that this girl was anxiously awaiting his arrival, she appeared to be quite surprised to see him. What was even more surprising was her astonishing beauty and gracious presence. We all had the same initial thought—"Wow! She is too good for this dude."

However, she seemed overwhelmed with joy to see Cicero, who escorted her our way and introduced us as his boys from The D. Her name was Ashley and she was a beautiful southern belle from Charleston, South Carolina. After some small talk with us, they retreated to a small room to be alone.

As we waited, Steve, Marco, and I all admitted that we were amazed at Cicero's ability to date a girl that fine. We speculated about what kind of lies he must have told her to pull off that stunt. Even more curiously, we could not understand why Cicero was trying to be a player when he had a girl like that in his pocket.

Meanwhile, it was not lost on us that we were on the premises of a women's college. With Cicero occupied, we took the opportunity to explore the small campus. After about an hour of exploration and willful conspicuousness, we returned to Ashley's dorm and found Cicero and Ashley standing on the steps.

Ashley was wiping her face where tears were still running down her cheeks. We were all wondering why Mr. Mouth didn't share with us whatever was so devastating to his girlfriend.

Marco jokingly said, "He just broke up with her."

Steve replied "That boy ain't never breaking up with that girl. Never."

We stopped a few yards short to give them some privacy. Cicero hugged her and gave a kiss on the cheek. Then, he left her standing there and started walking towards us.

The situation was uncomfortable, and it did not seem like the right time to say anything to Cicero. As the four of us walked silently toward the car, Marco awkwardly remarked that she looked as though she was going to kill herself. Cicero announced flatly that he had just broken up with her.

"WHAT!?" we all burst out a bit too loud for the discretion the situation called for. That news was more shocking than seeing Ashley for the first time.

The drama that I had just witnessed between Ashley and Cicero was quite remarkable. She did not yell expletives at Cicero. There was no pretension that her heart was not hurting. There was no hollow bluster about how she could find another guy any time she wanted to. Rather, her emotion radiated in the most genuinely feminine way that I had ever seen.

It was evident to us that she wasn't losing all that much and that Cicero could be easily replaced. Heck, there were three volunteer replacements in the car with him. We truly were in a different world. As we rode home, my thoughts turned back to the city of my birth.

The contrast between Ashley and many of the girls that I had interacted with in Detroit was striking. In particular, the difference between Ashley and the Sack-Chasers from Ram's Horn could not have been more glaring.

We were young men from Detroit who suddenly found ourselves in a world where a girl as pretty, intelligent, and gracious as Ashley stood on a doorstep crying because her broke, lying, two and three-timing, careless, now ex-boyfriend was riding off in the passenger seat of his friend's ride, like a scrub.

Maybe it was the thought of missing out on the false world that his lies often presented that led to her tears. Or, maybe it was the thought of missing out on the opportunity to see him reach his true potential as a college student that lead to her tears. I truly don't know *what it was* but somehow, despite dating a broke, average-looking guy, she saw his future absence as something worth seriously crying over.

Hell, if a death row inmate broke up with his pen-pal girlfriend, I would not be surprised if she cried. But, for some reason, their relationship represented more to me than just some guy breaking up with his girlfriend. Their break up somehow made me more aware of the deficiencies in my old community's value system compared to my new community. And, that very night, I decided that I could never live in Detroit again.

*

Virginia Beach

Although my late stage interest in high school academics is what got me into college, I didn't carry that interest in academics *to college.* As the first few days turned into the first few weeks of my freshman year, my weak interest in academics only weakened further. I went to every class, but my mind was always on what there was to do *after class*.

Cicero was always around. Although he was a year ahead of us, we were all the same age because he had been double-promoted. Moreover, he acted like our younger brother who we always had to keep in check.

Labor Day weekend had arrived and we needed something to do. Steve, Marco, and I sat in our dorm room wondering which college to visit to party. Suddenly, we could hear voices in the hallway outside our room greeting Cicero, and a moment later he was in our room delivering what sounded simultaneously like a plea and a command, "Yo, what y'all doing? Nothing, right? Let's go to Virginia Beach for the weekend!"

It had become a tradition that on Labor Day weekend students from black colleges descend on Virginia Beach in droves and just party the whole weekend.

"Labor Day weekend at Virginia Beach was where I met Ashley. Just imagine all those shorties in bikinis," Cicero said.

He didn't need to say anything else to convince me. I screamed, "Yeah, let's go!"

We packed our bags, put on our Detroit Tiger's gear, jumped in the Civic, and headed to Virginia Beach. A few hours later, we arrived on the main strip, where cars were cruising and black college students filled the sidewalks walking, laughing, and having a great time. It was an unbelievable sight: guys and girls walking in bathing suits without a care in the world except for the opposite sex.

Back in Detroit, you'd see thousands of young, black people every summer cruising along Jefferson Avenue—which Cicero mistakenly called "Washington Avenue"—and hanging out at Belle Isle. What made Virginia Beach so special was the positive vibe that was in the air.

In Detroit, you were always on edge, worried someone might start a fight or pull out a gun. There was a constant tension flowing under any fun in Detroit, so constant that it became unnoticeable. However, within the context of Virginia Beach's carefree, blissful atmosphere, our natural state of tension became painfully obvious to us and others. This protective, apprehensive kind of guard we wore so automatically in Detroit was out-of-place and unnecessary here.

The feeling only intensified once we parked and exited the car and started walking in what could be described as a happy parade of young black people. I had not been surrounded by so many carefree, happy, blissful black people since I lived in the projects as a child. People in Virginia Beach would notice us in our Detroit gear and greet us with a warm "Hey! What's up, Detroit?" Other Detroiters made the extra effort to squeeze through the crowd and greet us with Detroit's unique greeting of "What up, doe!"

In this parade, Cicero was talking to every other girl that walked by. He was in politician mode, shaking hands with guys and girls alike. Forget social butterfly, this guy was a social swarm of locusts.

As we walked northward, someone pointed out that there were three other guys across the street dressed just like us, in Detroit Tigers gear. We just acknowledged that those guys had great taste and kept walking. When we

114

arrived at the end of the strip, we crossed the street and headed back the way we came.

Eventually, we came to a parking lot in front of a two-story motel. The motel sat about thirty yards back from the sidewalk. There was a crowd of people outside along the first floor, as well as a bunch of people having a great time on the second story balcony. We could hear them chanting the chorus from a popular rap song by Boogie Down Productions: "*I say, the bridge is over, the bridge is over, biddy-bye-bye! The bridge is over, the bridge is over, hey, hey!*"

We slowed our pace to observe. They were chanting in unison, their hands swaying in the air from left to right. It reminded us of our pep rallies back in high school.

Cicero jumped up in the air and yelled, "Man! New York is hype!"

Then, I heard a faint chant coming from somewhere within the crowd. Cicero squinted and said that he could hear it, too. People in front of the motel started moving over to the left and to the right, eventually revealing our Detroit duplicates alone in the middle.

Suddenly, this chant started to wane. We walked closer, and by the time we got to the halfway point between the street and the motel, the only thing clearly audible was coming from the three guys in Detroit Tiger's jerseys. They were chanting, "New York ain't shit! New York ain't shit! New York ain't shit! New York ain't shit!"

I thought to myself, leave it to people from Detroit to come to paradise and start a fight. It was as if we were witnessing someone spray-painting over a beautiful piece of museum art. The New Yorkers were in a state of bewilderment and we were all mortified. Except for Cicero. He was ecstatic.

"Hell yeah! Detroit is in the house! Fuck New York!" he exclaimed a bit too loudly for our comfort.

"Shut up, dumb ass. You don't even know how many people from New York might be over there," Marco scolded.

Steve said, "Let's get the hell out of here before someone from New York starts shooting people with Detroit Tigers jerseys on." At that, we dragged Cicero away and continued walking.

When night came, the streets swarmed with cars and the foot- traffic on the sidewalk became more dense. Along with the increase in black bodies was an increase in the police presence.

There were polite requests for us to stay on the sidewalk and out of the streets by some officers and menacing and threatening commands from other officers. There were officers on horseback using their horses in aggressive sweeps to keep us on the sidewalks.

It was obvious that there were too many people to reasonably expect everyone to be able to stay on the side walk. There were just too many people. Before long, we saw a cop knock a young lady down with his horse, yelling, "Stay on the sidewalk!" It was obvious that her intentions had been to remain on the sidewalk.

This, and other acts of aggression by some of the cops toward an otherwise happy yet rambunctious crowd of black college kids, made the police seem like racist pigs trying to herd black people.

As the demands from the police grew more and more intense, I felt the tension that we always carried tamped down inside us, suddenly creep back up. Not just for the Detroiters—but for everyone in the crowd.

Suddenly, we heard the explosion of glass breaking somewhere ahead of us. Immediately, the cop who knocked the young lady down took off toward the sound. The smooth movement of the crowd became more agitated. Something was going on up ahead, but we could not see what was happening. Then, there was another burst of breaking glass, followed by screaming and yelling.

Suddenly, as if someone had dropped a grenade, the organized flock of people suddenly exploded into complete pandemonium. People left the sidewalks and were running all over the streets, girls were screaming, guys were yelling, cops were chasing everyone. Glass from retail shops was shattering all around.

Within a minute, a happy beach vacation atmosphere exploded into a full-blow and very dangerous riot.

Steve turned to us and said with an urgent steadiness in his voice, "It is time to go."

"Hold on. Let's find out what happened first," Cicero pleaded.

"If you want to stay, you can stay. But I'm going back to my car and getting the hell out of here."

117

"I'll see y'all back at school," Cicero responded, unfazed.

"Huh?" I asked. "Just how do you plan on getting back to school?"

"Don't worry, homie. I'm going to stick around and have some fun."

"Okay, bye." Steve had called Cicero's bluff.

But it was no bluff. Cicero insisted that we leave him behind to enjoy the riot. Marco, Steve, and I were a lot more concerned about Cicero's safety than he was, but we could not force him to see reason. The three of us jogged back to the car and drove a safe distance away from the strip.

Once the mayhem had long vanished from our rearview mirror, and we had quieted down, Marco was suddenly overcome with emotion.

"Black folks just can't have shit!" he vented. Steve and I agreed.

We listened to the radio to try and find out what happened. But there was no news on the riot, so we all dozed off to sleep for a few hours.

In the wee hours of the morning, we woke feeling no less demoralized and drove back to school. We knew Cicero had arrived back on campus Monday when we heard people outside our dorm room greeting him as he walked down the hallway. He entered the room without invitation, as per usual, to interrupt our normally scheduled *whatever*. Cicero claimed to have made his way back by hanging out with some girls he knew from North Carolina A&T and that they had just dropped him off.

After a monologue about some romantic encounters, he got around to telling us what we were really interested in hearing about. According to him, there was a full-on race riot and the center of the storm had been just a few feet ahead of where we were walking. Apparently, the cops on horseback deliberately knocked down one too many sisters, and the brothers just lost it.

Cicero compared the black Virginia Beach party and the predominately white Dayton Beach Spring break party that he attended the year before. His conclusion was that the rowdiness of those at Virginia Beach did not exceed the rowdiness of the white college students who flocked to Dayton Beach. The cops' actions had nothing to do with our behavior. Condemning the cops as racist was as obvious to us as the blue sky we were under.

Although brief in duration, I got to experience a black paradise. But sadly, some black assholes from Detroit, in effect, took a dump on the streets of that black paradise by trying to intimidate black New Yorkers who were just having fun. Their ridiculousness was followed by actions of white asshole cops being overly aggressive, all of which lead eventually to a riot. Both played a part in destroying the black paradise.

The rest of my first semester at NCCU consisted of an unwavering dedication to partying and drinking which was inversely proportional to my attention to my schoolwork. I also found myself complaining more and more about America's racist society.

At the end of my first semester, I had to tell my parents that I had a D+ average, and that I had made some really good friends. Thanks to my black friend Cicero from the white suburbs, I had plenty of stories to tell. But, the only story I told my parents over the phone when asked about my grades was that I'd do better the next semester.

119

They were furious. If I did not straighten up, they were going to pull me out of school. I promised that I would be more focused, and my parents prayed that I would have the strength to resist temptation. But, alas, accountability was not on my radar, so it was easy to blame things on the Devil.

The second semester started and ended like the first: with me drinking and partying all the time. I squandered an opportunity of a lifetime to get an education and had thrown it away like an empty 40-ounce bottle of malt liquor. When the last day of my first year as a college student came, I jumped in Steve's car and headed home with a heavy heart.

*

You're grown now

I arrived home in Detroit to the proud smiles of my family. Everyone asked how I did in school. Though I was terrified, I would nonchalantly say I believed I did okay. Secretly, I was scared I would get kicked out of school and forced to spend the rest of my existence in Detroit. Although Detroit could be conceived of as a geophysical black cocoon, I preferred to be in a black cocoon in North Carolina, where there were no dangerous thugs or sack-chasing women.

In Detroit, not only would I have to deal with those two dynamics, but I would also have to expand my wits and energy simply trying to avoid situations where I could either lose my freedom due to incarceration or lose my life itself.

120

In the meantime, I went around visiting my old friends: Keith, Kevin, and the others. It was apparent that they were living the life I was trying to avoid. Whenever I asked someone what they had been up to since I had left, the answer was always the same: "Nothing." I began to hate the very sound of the word.

None of the homeboys I visited were doing anything promising or productive. Instead, they kept busy by complaining about the lack of jobs for blacks. Even if the jobs weren't leaving Detroit like roaches fleeing the light, they believed they would not get them because of institutional racism.

The only things I'd apparently missed while being away from Detroit were endless stories of people being shot, Sack-Chasers, more girls getting pregnant, and more brothers going to jail.

On the other hand, I brought story after story of sweet-hearted girls, partying, and buying stuff with the assortment of credit cards I got just for being a college student. Not wanting to sound like I was bragging, I threw in a few complaints about having to go to class hung over.

The longer I was I back in Detroit, the more I became less enamored with my college stories. Detroit did not change and was not going to. The prospect of being stuck there for the foreseeable future was deeply upsetting. My stories were sounding more and more like cruel jokes I was telling at my own expense. Two thoughts kept echoing inside my head: I should have studied more and I have to get the hell out of Detroit.

Around the first week of June, my grades made it to my door in an envelope addressed to my mother. The news was terrible: I was on academic probation with a dismal GPA of 1.71.

For my mother, it must have been like finding out she had been a victim of fraud. I felt thoroughly ashamed, but the disappointment my mother felt must have been worse. She had taken out loans that she could not afford to send me to school. I repaid her sacrifice by becoming a professional partier.

Her disappointment quickly gave way to anger, and she really let me have it.

"Andre, I wish I could give you a beating and put you on punishment until you turn twenty-five or however long it takes you to pay all the money back that I just wasted!"

"But I can get my grades up and do better next semester," I pleaded desperately.

"You are not going back down there. You are going to college right here, and you will get on the dean's list and repay the nine thousand dollars I just wasted on you" she screamed.

"But my classes were not that hard, except for math," I explained. "The problem was that I could not adjust to the responsibilities that came with all of that freedom. I lost it. I was like one of those sheltered kids you hear about."

She responded with an exasperated sigh. My stepfather, who was also there, said nothing.

"But now I know how to handle the freedom. I want the responsibility of that freedom. Please don't take that away from me," I implored.

My mother just rolled her eyes up toward the ceiling and stared at it. My stepfather folded his arms tightly and kept mum. Unsure of where I stood, I upped the ante.

"I want to overcome my past failure. I'll do everything humanly possible to get my GPA up to a minimum GPA of 3.5," I proclaimed.

There was an uncomfortably long moment of silence, and then my parents got up and walked into the kitchen. I had no idea where the chips were going to fall. A couple of hours later, they summoned me into the kitchen where my mother delivered the verdict: They agreed that I should go back and redeem myself. I had won that battle.

After I finished groveling to them, I immediately put my plan into action. I went back to Ram's Horn and got my old job back on the weekends. Then I got a second job as a nighttime janitor during the week, as well as a third job as a part-time merchandiser for 7-Up Bottling Company. The fear of being eternally marooned in Detroit turned into the strongest inspiration I had ever felt in my life. Every day and every interaction with someone who had a hard luck story motivated me to work as hard as I could to escape.

At the end of the following week, another envelope came in the mail. This time it was from the Financial Aid Office of NCCU, and it was addressed to me. Due to my GPA falling below 2.0, I was now ineligible for financial aid. The die was cast. My parents could not afford to write a check for my tuition, so I was no longer a college student.

It is true that fear is the greatest motivator. I was scared of a life in Detroit. Even if I couldn't come up with the money for tuition for NCCU, I made up my mind that I was *not staying in Detroit*, no matter what.

After receiving this death blow from NCCU's financial aid office, I called to ask what my options were. I was advised to write a letter asking for an exception, though the decision would most likely be made after the start of the fall semester. However, I would be allowed to register for classes and attend the first two weeks of class without a decision on my case.

The alternative was to pay several thousand dollars for tuition for the first semester. My parents were living paycheck-to-paycheck with little to no savings. So handing over four grand in cash was not an option. I sat down and wrote a heartfelt letter begging for another chance.

If I could not get financial aid, I would just work and pay rent somewhere off campus long enough to establish in-state residency. That way, I could pay the five-hundred-dollar tuition bill for North Carolina residents. I could eventually recapture the title of student by trading my Detroit residency for a Durham residency. Despite the way students acted towards them, I was actually looking forward to becoming a Durmite.

*

By mid-July, I thought that I had saved up enough money to buy a piece-of-crap car. I took seven hundred dollars and walked to a used car dealership near my house. My expectations were meager, to begin with, but

124

my seven hundred dollars was still not enough to buy anything on the lot. The salesman asked if I would like to try and finance a car, but I adamantly turned him down. After all, I just needed something to get me to school. He suggested that I go to a new car dealer because some people traded in cars so terrible that the dealer would be unable to resell them for a profit. Usually, new car dealers would send those cars to an auction, and there was a chance that I could catch a car between trade-in and auction.

I took his advice and called Steve to ask if he could take me to look at cars. Together, we visited several dealers. Because Steve's car made him appear to fit the profile of a drug dealer rather than the struggling college student he really was, we had no problem finding sales associates eager to help us. After hearing the same story told by several different salesmen at various dealerships, my hopes of buying a car that day were dimming.

The last dealership of the day was a Pontiac-GMC truck dealer. Tired and disappointed from the day's activities, I told the first salesman to come our way that I had seven hundred dollars to buy a car. Before I could say that I was looking for a car that was going to auction the salesman started bombarding me with qualifying questions.

"What will the car be used for?"

"I just need it to get me to North Carolina, so I can go to school," I replied.

"Are you a student?"

"Yes."

"Are you working right now?"

"Yes. In fact, I'm working three jobs."

Upon hearing that, his pupils dilated. "Will this be your first time buying a car?"

"Yes."

"How old are you?"

"Nineteen."

"Do you have any credit cards?"

"Yes. I have a Mastercard, Visa, and American Express."

"Great! We should be able to get you in a car today," the salesman said as if to congratulate me. Then he motioned that we should walk and talk.

"Wow, that's great," I said. "Because all the other salesmen laughed at me when I said I wanted to buy a car for seven hundred dollars."

The salesman stopped in his tracks. "Wait. Are you trying to purchase a car that costs seven hundred bucks?"

"Yes."

Without skipping a beat, he said, "You can't, but I'll show you what you can buy."

He guided us past the cars on the lot and into the showroom. There she was, sparkling in the center of the room. It was a blindingly bright red, brand new, small pickup truck with a ground effect kit and flood lights. It looked like a show car.

The salesman proceeded to tell me that because I was a first-time buyer, I qualified for a first-time buyer's rebate. Also, because I was a college student, I qualified for a student rebate. And, because it was a new vehicle, I qualified for a new car rebate. The clincher was that I had three jobs and three credit cards so I would qualify for financing. Plus, the rebates would take care of my down payment and leave me with a tiny monthly payment.

Steve and I stood there in total disbelief. As if my lust was not already obvious, the salesman asked if I liked the truck. I was pondering an excuse any excuse to say no, but he quickly asked if I'd drive it home if he could get the financing arranged.

I called a timeout—I had not come to the dealership looking for a show car. I came looking for a bucket to get me from Detroit to North Carolina, and then from my apartment to campus every day. Apparently, I wouldn't be able to save up and buy a cheap, reliable used car before school started. However, I could buy a reliable, brand-new truck that would cost me nothing that day.

A dilemma confronted me: walk away without a car and no way to get back and forth from school and work in North Carolina or drive off with a truck that would make any drug dealer proud and stimulate any Sack-Chaser.

Even through the ever-cautious Steve tried to talk me out of it, I reasoned that I had to get out of Detroit and I would not have the time to save up enough money for a reliable used car by the time school started. I reasoned further that in North Carolina, the truck would just be a symbol of affluence, rather than one of crime and community destruction. I told the salesman to see what he could do regarding financing, and a few hours later, I shed the image of a struggling college student for one of a drug dealer.

127

I was handed a set of keys to a brand-new truck with a manual transmission and no radio or air conditioning. In all my excitement, I had not thought about the fact that the truck had a manual transmission. I'd spontaneously taken on a five-year commitment to make payments on a truck I did not know how to drive. I couldn't tell if it was brave or stupid.

With a few words of encouragement and instructions from the salesman, I drove the truck off the lot and up to the curb of Telegraph Road, a thoroughfare with a speed limit of 45 mph that most people took as a suggestion. I waited until traffic was clear, then jerked my way onto the road and learned how to drive my new truck.

Several hours after I bought the truck and half a gas tank later I arrived home. Needless to say, my parents were shocked and beyond upset. However, I gave another confidence-inspiring speech about my determination not to let anything or anyone get in the way of me attending NCCU. They seemed to buy it, conceding, "You're grown now."

*

Church: The Drug Spot

When I pulled into Kevin's driveway, he was standing there talking to his mother. Upon noticing me, his mom put her hands on her hips and glared at the car, half surprised and half confused. Meanwhile, Kevin broke into a grin. I was no longer on the bench. I was in the game.

"Hey!" he greeted happily. "Whose is this?"

"It's mine."

He immediately proffered some constructive criticism.

"Player, you are doing it wrong. You need some rims and a sound system for this truck."

"I would agree with you, but it's just a vehicle to get me to school."

He dismissed my statement with a "Yeah, yeah, whatever."

Kevin always knew someone who knew someone. This time, it was a guy desperate for cash that sold him an incredible sound system for a steal. That is because it was stolen. Kevin led me into his basement, where he showed me an Alpine cassette deck with a detachable face, an amplifier, and a speaker box with two fifteen-inch subwoofers, four horns, and four tweeters.

"Give me six hundred dollars, and it's yours," he said. "I'll even help you install it."

I explained, "I love it, man, but I can't afford it. All I have is seven hundred dollars plus a few more checks to come. I'll need every penny for an apartment and school stuff."

"Yeah, yeah, whatever," he dismissed again. "Andre, I'll give you an eight ball of crack to sell."

"What?" I exclaimed. That escalated quickly.

"I'm selling because everybody is buying."

"Man, I don't know anyone who wants to buy crack!"

"Just think about it, Andre."

"There is nothing to think about, Kevin. I don't know any crack heads."

"Well, you can give me six hundred dollars for this sound system, or one hundred and fifty dollars for cocaine that I'll turn into crack. You sell the crack, give me six hundred dollars from your profits, and you can keep the rest."

"No deal, Kevin."

"Well, just let me know."

The following Sunday, I went to church for the first time since returning from school. Not to praise God, but to get praised for my new truck. To my surprise, several of the teenage girls were pregnant, unmarried, and listening to the same sermon about how premarital sex is a sin.

During church, I started talking to a young guy named Rob that I had not seen in about two years. In between choir songs, Rob leisurely mentioned that he was selling drugs. Recognizing an opportunity, I mentioned Kevin's proposal. Rob told me to get him the crack and said he would have it sold in a few hours.

I left church to hand my cousin Kevin one hundred and fifty dollars, and he went into his kitchen and started cooking crack in his parent's mini-mansion. I risked incarceration by transporting crack cocaine in a truck that screamed to anyone in Detroit, especially the cops, "I'm a drug dealer!"

With luck on my side and stupidity in my head, I delivered the drugs to Rob that evening. Rob handed me six hundred dollars the following Sunday, in church, of all places. That Sunday night, I had the most fantastic sound system my ears had ever heard.

Let's Do It Again

The day to leave for NCCU arrived. As I passed the city limits blasting hip-hop music over my new sound system, I said goodbye to Detroit and its crime, drugs, Sack-Chasers, and hopelessness. It was time to say hello to opportunity, friendly people, and a better life.

Dee had timed his arrival at Durham's Greyhound bus station with my arrival. We had a mutual friend who lived close to Chidley Hall named Shirley. She agreed to let me store my kicker box and our bodies on her couch and floor until we found a place to rent. Over an impressive dinner Shirley prepared for us, I told the story of how I acquired the truck and sound system to my captive audience. Then we went to sleep to tackle housing and school registration in the morning.

Registering for class was simple for the both of us, and financial aid was almost as simple for Dee. However, it was the beginning of a long nightmare for me that would not end for months. On the bright side, we were able to find an apartment near campus, and our limited skill set allowed us to secure temp work at an IBM factory through a temp agency.

The rest of the Detroit crew made their way down to Durham on a Thursday. That evening, we drove down the street in front of the student union. Steve led the way with Marco in the car, followed by Dee and me in the truck. The street was like a valley with tall, women-only dorms on each side.

131

Acoustically, it was perfect. We drove through the valley, letting everyone on campus know that The D was in the house.

NCCU had never experienced anything like my rolling hip-hop concert. We eventually arrived at a parking lot across from the student union and set off an impromptu party. People, including security guards, came running from all directions saying that they could clearly hear my music all over campus. The security guards were enjoying themselves as well, though they said that I would have to shut it down at 10 PM. All in all, it seemed that everyone had a fantastic time.

Friday night was more of the same. When we arrived on campus, there was already a crowd waiting for us, and it seemed to have doubled in size compared to the night before. Due to the size of the crowd, we were being watched closely by security. They warned that some of the people in the crowd were not students, so we should be careful.

Be careful of what? There was no way I would have a few hundred people engulfing me and my sound system in Detroit. But since we were the only ones from Detroit that we knew of in Durham, I figured everything was safe. And it was. We had a great time mingling, bobbing our heads to the music, and fielding questions about Cicero's whereabouts. We all were starting to wonder if he was coming back to school. Maybe he had gotten kicked out and did not want to tell anyone. We had no idea. We just knew that it was strange that no one had heard from him and that he had not arrived on campus yet.

While the first two affairs had been essentially impromptu, by the time Saturday evening came around, we had actually prepared for these festivities. The Detroit crew wanted to exceed expectations, so we planned our playlist in advance and had the tapes lined up in the sequence we would play them. The dope Civic with the ragtop and the bright red truck with the sounds arrived on the scene to even more fanfare. We drove through the valley of dorms and stopped in the parking lot. Music was blasting from the kicker box, and life was great.

Just when we thought things couldn't get better, out of nowhere a brand-new, shiny, black Mustang GT 5.0 appeared. It was moving recklessly fast through the crowd. The car stopped right behind my truck in the center of the crowd, and Cicero jumped out like a jack in the box.

"What's up!" he screamed, trying to be heard over my music. He ran over and gave me a hug. "I couldn't be the only one from Detroit without a fresh ride." He gave high fives all around.

Dee was the first to ask with a doubtful tone, "Whose car is it, Cicero?"

"It's mine!"

"Man, your parents, hooked you up," I said with more than a hint of jealousy.

"My parents don't even know I have it!"

"How did you get it?" Dee asked.

With the volume of a battle cry, he yelled over the music, "Selling drugs!"

133

We immediately dismissed the statement as a joke.

Before the usual shutdown time, a security guard walked up to me and said I had to end the party because the sound was disturbing the residents in the neighborhood. Without hesitation, I turned the music off, and people started to disperse to various dorm room parties on campus. I wanted to attend as well, but I could not go into a dorm and leave my sound system unattended. Dee suggested that I drop off the kicker box at Shirley's place. So we did, and with that out of the way, we immediately drove back to the parking lot. The rest of the Detroit crew was waiting on us.

As soon as we got out of the truck, we heard a *POP POP POP* and then screaming. It was gunfire. People were running directly at us in hysterics. "Hell yeah!" Cicero shouted. Then, he immediately started running toward the sound of the gunfire.

Before he could get very far, Steve grabbed him and said, "You *ain't from Detroit*, are you? You run *away* from sounds like that, *not towards* sounds like that."

When people got to the parking lot, they stopped running and started talking. A guy had just been shot in front of one of the administration buildings. No one seemed to know the shooter or the victim, but everyone assumed it was a Durmite who did the shooting. After a few minutes, we heard sirens and decided it was okay to go check out what was happening. When we arrived at the scene, there was a crowd of students encircling someone on the ground. Some were crying, some were screaming, and some were praying.

While the paramedics quickly hooked up a machine to the person on the ground, the police attempted to push the crowd back. The screams, prayers, and cries blended into an incoherent wave of sound. Yet, the sound of the machine was somehow still distinguishable through the ruckus. We all listened as the heartbeat slowed, then slowed some more, bu-bum, bu-bum, beeeeeeeep.

The paramedics continued to try and revive the man as they loaded him into the ambulance. We could see that it was a young, black male, who people were saying had just arrived on campus. Others were cursing the shooter, and others still were praying. Most people just stood there in disbelief.

As the police and campus security broke up the crowd, information about the victim began to circulate. He had transferred from Hampton University as a sophomore and had just arrived in Durham that day. Like all the students around my truck, my music drew him out of his dorm to hang out.

However, before he arrived at his destination, he got into an altercation with several Durmites also headed to the party at my truck. In the end, two black males lost their lives. One was now dead, and the other would spend his life in jail.

*

Life as a Durmite

The first week of school, I went to classes during the day and assembled computer parts at IBM during the night. The pay was enough to cover my rent, car payment, and food, but not enough to pay for tuition. Though I dutifully attended class and took all of my work very seriously, the answer to my petition for financial aid did not come within the two-week window. I could no longer attend classes.

It was official. I was a Durmite, and I was barely making ends meet. However, not having to study freed me up to live my utopian college life. When I got home from work, I would have nothing to do but look for something to get into, and Cicero always availed. Cicero caught up with Dee and me on a Saturday in early October. He invited us to go with him, his two cousins who just started at NCCU, and our mutual friends Phil and Brad to a party at Virginia Union University.

After a few hours of driving in a caravan of cars, we arrived on campus in the late afternoon. We hung out with some people that Cicero had previously met at some other party at some other school in some other state. We ended up at a dorm room party and had a very good time, but struck out on finding housing for the night. So, at around two in the morning, we decided to make the trek back home to Durham.

As Cicero led our caravan along the highway, Dee and I noticed him yelling out of his window to a girl traveling next to him in the only other car on the visible highway in either direction.

Not again, I thought. He was attempting to have a full-on conversation with this girl on the highway at about 50 miles an hour. Suddenly, Cicero was making gestures with his hand indicating that he wanted her to pull off the highway. At this point, Dee asked me to pull alongside Cicero's car.

136

"Hey, do you know her?" he asked.

"No."

"We're tired, man," Dee moaned.

"It's okay. I gotta get gas anyway."

"Ugh."

As we continued bitching and moaning about Cicero and his efforts to meet every person on the planet, the girl's right blinker started blinking, as did Cicero's, and then Phil's, and finally mine. We pulled into the gas station. When the girl exited the car, we went from a state of annoyance to a state of utter disbelief.

Dee was suddenly fully awake and at attention. His eyes were glued to the girl as he blurted, "What the...? Goddamn! Do you see this chick?" "Hell yeah. How could I not?" I responded, thunderstruck. She was stunningly beautiful. We instantly forgave Cicero.

What had seemed like a monumental waste of everyone's time just seconds earlier now all made sense. Cicero introduced everyone, and because she was so cute, we didn't mind waiting to see where things were going. We started speculating that the girl had to be another one of Cicero's many cousins who lived in the South. There was no way a girl looking like that would pull off the highway in the middle of nowhere for a total stranger being followed by two other cars. But Cicero's cousin's shot that theory down. She wasn't a relative.

Within a few minutes, Cicero came over to us to give us the report. "Yo, shorty is going down to Camp Lejeune. She's being deployed to Desert

Storm. She started off in D.C. and says she's tired. I told her she could crash at my place for a few hours and get some sleep."

We were staring at Cicero waiting in vain for him to retract his statement. Finally, Dee asked, "Cicero, where did you tell her you lived?" We all knew that Cicero was sleeping in his local girlfriend Jazz's bed, or on Steve and Marco's couch. This was because all of his room and board money that his parents sent him was used to pay all the guys he owed money to in Chidley hall.

Cicero had passed himself off as me to his new acquaintance, telling her he was roommates with Dee and that he had a super king- size bed that four people could sleep in without touching one another. He chose to be me instead of Dee because he suspected, as we all did, that Dee's girlfriend Tonya would be waiting at home for him.

I protested, "Hell no, Cicero! I'm tired. I'm sleeping in my bed. You can tell her whatever you want. But, if she is sleeping in my bed, she will be sleeping in it with me."

"*Come on*, Andre," he pleaded.

I stood fast. "No. You guys can sleep on the couches in the living room."

Phil and Brad chimed in "You know we don't have room." His cousins stated the obvious "We can't sneak her into Chidley."

With a soft voice, Cicero said "OK. Forget it," and headed off toward the girl.

138

About forty minutes later, we arrived at my apartment. As we got out of our cars, I could hear Cicero being Cicero. "Yeah, I have a huge bed, so don't worry." Before he was able to tell too many more lies, I walked over to the girl and welcomed her to our home. "I understand that Cicero may have offered you my bed. You are welcome to sleep in it. It takes up ninety percent of the bedroom and can sleep four people comfortably," I explained. She looked at Cicero with a suspicious eye and answered, "Okay." Cicero stood there like he had just been caught with his pants down.

Phil and Brad agreed to drop off Cicero's cousins on their way home. After we all had said goodbye, the three of us led the girl into our apartment. It seemed that we were more nervous than she was. She acted as if it was perfectly normal for her to be walking into an apartment with three guys she just met on a highway.

Dee's girlfriend Tonya wasn't there, and Dee headed straight to the answering machine located in the hallway between our bedrooms, expecting just a few messages. Just as I was going to show our quest where the bathroom was, Dee nearly screamed, "Dre, there are eleven messages on the machine! Some of these have to be for you too." He called me over to the machine. We listened anxiously to the playback while Cicero entertained his new friend.

7:00 pm: "Cicero, this is Steve. Where are you? Kay just came down from A&T to see you."

8:120 pm: "Cicero, this is Marco. Do not come over here without calling first! Jazz just showed up looking for you!"

8:30 pm: "It's Steve. Hey, Cicero, shit is bad, man. Kay went into the kitchen, got a knife, and went after Jazz. Marco had to separate them."

9:50 pm: "It's Marco. Don't come over here, man. They are not mad at each other anymore. They are mad at you!"

10:11 pm: "Dre, you need to find Cicero. These girls are talking about kicking his ass when he gets here. They won't leave."

10:55 pm: "Cicero, where the fuck you at, man? Your Durmite chick just showed up."

11:21 pm: "It's Steve. Tell Cicero he better skip town. The Durmite just told it all."

1:03 am: "It's Marco. These chicks won't leave. Dre and Dee, if you see Cicero, tell him I'm going to kick his trifling ass."

As Cicero was telling the girl more lies, I pulled him out of my bedroom. "Sounds like your ass is in trouble," I warned.

Dee and I watched his face as he listened to the messages.

With every sound indicating a new message, from the machine, came a "shiiiit!" from Cicero. His panic escalated with every beep.

"Your ass finally got caught," Dee said.

"Shit!" Cicero rushed over to the girl and said that he had to go because of an emergency. He just left her there with us and ran out the door.

I called Steve and told him that we just got back, that Cicero got the messages, and that he was either on his way over there or getting the hell out of town. Steve told me that the Durmite had left, but that Kay and Jazz were still there waiting on him. Then he recounted the conversation between the three women:

Apparently, they were just kicking it with Kay when Jazz came over. Kay opened the door, and Jazz was somewhat startled to see a girl answer our door. She said "Hi" and asked everyone in earshot if Cicero was home. Kay asked who she was and Jazz asked who she was, and things got out of hand immediately. Just when they'd gotten the girls to settle down, there was another knock on the door. They all thought it was Cicero. Steve thought that it would be best if he opened the door. But it wasn't Cicero, it was Cicero's Durmite. She immediately asked, "Where Cicero at?"

So Kay and Jazz asked in kind, "Who are you?"

With eyeballs bulging and the attitude of the hood rat she was, the Durmite responded, "Who the fuck are you? And where is Cicero?"

"What do you want with Cicero? Who are you?" Kay asked, taken aback.

"I'm his girlfriend....well, kind of."

"Me, too," Kay responded, sounding unwittingly foolish.

Without so much as a blink, the Durmite asked, "Which one are you? Kay or Jazz?"

"Why do you know our names?"

"Oh, he told me all about you. Kay is paying the car note, and Jazz is paying for the insurance. I give him gas money and sex every now and then. Do y'all know about the teacher in Alabama? She co-signed on the loan so he could get the car."

141

The Durmite broke it down so matter-of-factly that Kay appeared unsure of whether to be mad or appreciative of her candor. The entire episode sounded preposterous. Under normal circumstances, I would have accused Steve of kidding around. But all manner of tomfoolery was plausible if Cicero was involved. Steve then summed it up, "Dre, we all stood there in silence. None of us could believe it. The Durmite told them *everything*. She said she knew all about Cicero's scheming, but was cool with it. And then when she was walking out, she said to tell Cicero to call her because she had a feeling he is going to be pretty lonely.'"

Indeed, it turned out that Cicero skipped town. We did not see him for the next three weeks. He camped out at his cousin's place in Wilmington, North Carolina. Eventually, he was able to show his face in Durham again safely, but NC A&T would be off-limits from then on.

*

At the time, my level of maturity and amount of life experiences led me to an oversimplified opinion of those involved in that Cicero fiasco. Back then, I had concluded that Cicero had mad game, that he deserved the pimp of the year award, and that those girls were just stupid. Now as I reflect on that situation I have formulated a different opinion.

We all were regularly exposed to a bombardment of negative statistics concerning the lack of good black men for black women. Supporting evidence like a 5 to 1 girl to boy dorm ratio on campus and statements like, "there are

142

more black men in prison than in college," or that "one out of four black men will end up in the penal system," were commonly tossed about.

In a way, just being a free black man with a personality and a car was good enough for a complete stranger in the military, two undergraduate students, a teacher, and a hood-rat. The low standards that these women held Cicero to were acceptable standards in a society predicated on race—far from acceptable in a society predicated on skills, values, and social behavior. Cicero, the former honor roll student, was not a pimp to be put on a pedestal but a failure to be ostracized, rebuked, and incarcerated.

*

The Ticket

While Cicero found himself unofficially banned from North Carolina A&T, I was seeing a girl enrolled there named Angie. She was a sophomore and lived in the dorms, where privacy was often lacking. We spent most of our time together at my place on the weekends. I'd pick her up on Fridays and take her back to campus Sunday nights.

That routine was broken one weekend when Angie jumped in my truck with more books in her bags than clothes. The privacy she was seeking that weekend was for the purpose of studying for an exam—not spending time alone with me, as I'd hoped. I gave her all the privacy that I could but disturbed her just enough for her to contend that she needed to study all through Sunday night to do well on her exam. So, she needed me to take her home first thing Monday morning.

143

Monday morning arrived, and we were running behind schedule just enough to put her in jeopardy of missing her exam. So, I decided to literally destroy the speed limit *and* the eardrums of those on the highway.

Though the highway speed limit was fifty-five miles per hour, I was averaging close to ninety miles an hour as I tore up the far left lane. Trying to be safe at break neck speeds, I'd flash my high beams and fog lights at cars in front of me to signal them to get out of my path—as if my breaks had suddenly gone out.

Somewhere between Durham and Greensboro sat a highway patrolman in a Ford Mustang GT patrol car listening to his radio. He received a call from dispatch reporting a red truck heading his way, driving recklessly fast and flashing lights at cars ahead. He moved into position to catch me and succeeded. As I rolled to a stop on the side of the highway, I put the truck in park, turned off the engine and the radio. I set my hands on the steering wheel and looked over at Angie, who gave me an I-told-you-so look.

We sat quietly, as the patrolman came to the passenger side of the car.

"Ma'am, are you okay? Is this man taking you somewhere against your will?"

Her shock was apparent in her voice as she replied, "He's my boyfriend, and he was just trying to get me to school for an exam that I have to take."

The officer glanced over at me and asked for my license and registration with an authoritative voice. When I handed over the items, he briefly scanned them and muttered an "affirmative" to the voice coming from the speaker on his shoulder.

His voice took on a new intensity as he asked, "Do you have any drugs in this truck?"

"No," I replied. "Check if you want to but I'm just a college student. I don't mess with drugs."

Another patrol car pulled up behind his, after which he ordered me to step out of the vehicle. I did as I was told. Despite the anxiety of the situation, I couldn't help but ruminate on the fact that Angie had called me her boyfriend. The first officer on the scene led me to his car, where the other patrolman was waiting. The first patrolman asked me if I knew why I was being pulled over. Maybe the presence of the other patrolman put him at ease because his intensity level had fallen several notches. I took the opportunity to try to gain some favor with the cops.

With a guilty grin and shoulders hunched, I replied, "Was I going too slow?"

"Cute."

I was cuffed and sat in the front seat of the Mustang GT.

"You're lucky that you have a North Carolina driver's license. If you had an out-of-state license, I would take you to jail."

I replied, "I guess so. My girlfriend can't drive my truck, so I would have to get it towed as well."

All the while, I was fascinated with his patrol car. I started asking him about all the equipment. He seemed pretty interested in telling me about it and, pretty soon, I got around to asking him about the radio.

"Yeah," he said. "I listen to it and rock out a bit. In fact, that is what I was doing when I got the call. You passed someone, and they used their car phone to call the police on you. They said you were tailgating and flashing your lights and that the girl looked like she was in distress."

"What? I'll admit to speeding, but that's a lie. By the way, how fast did you clock me at?"

"Ninety-three, but I'm going to put eighty-nine, so I don't have to take you to jail for reckless driving."

"Thanks."

"But *you will* have to show up for court."

"That's fine with me," I replied. We soon parted ways with the patrolmen and continued on to NC A&T.

When the court date arrived, I drove to the little courthouse in the middle of "Nowhere," North Carolina. The clerk instructed me to sit down and wait until my name was called. My prayer that the patrolman would not show up and my case would be dismissed went unanswered. There he was: the poster boy for state patrol officers. He was white, clean-cut, uniform starched and pressed, and about thirty years old with one of those porn star mustaches.

Before my name was called, the name of a white guy in his Marine uniform was called. He got caught speeding by the same patrolman and was ticketed for doing eighty-nine miles per hour just like me.

146

The prosecutor presented the charges to the judge. The judge had a little back and forth with the Marine, where it was discovered that the Marine was from Michigan just like me. The marine pled not guilty, and then the prosecutor presented his evidence. The judge gave him the kind of scolding for speeding that you would expect a grandfather to give his rambunctious grandson for spilling milk. Before finding the marine guilty, the judge thanked the private first class for his service and then told him that because he was being deployed to Desert Storm, he would only be required to pay the court fee.

My case was next. How bad could it be? I'm not going to war, but I am from Michigan, and I am a college student. At least in my mind, I was a college student. The prosecutor read the charges with a noticeable sternness in his voice that was lacking in the prior case.

Then, I was asked, "How do you plead?" I just followed everyone else's lead and innocently replied, "Not guilty."

The prosecutor pulled out a copy of the ticket and read the patrolman's notation. "'Flashing lights and tailgating.' Your Honor, Mr. Davis was driving at extremely fast speeds in a new, red pickup truck, endangering the lives of the people on the highway. His behavior was so bad that someone used their car phone to call the police."

"Mr. Davis, what do you say in your defense?" the judge asked.

"Well, I was speeding, but I wasn't driving crazy. I flashed my lights to tell the people in front of me that I wanted to pass."

"So you admit to speeding?"

147

"Yes."

"Eighty-nine miles per hour in a fifty-five mile-per-hour zone?"

"Yes."

"Whose car were you driving?"

"It is my truck."

"What are you not guilty of?"

"Driving crazy."

"Well, Mr. Davis, in this county, driving that fast is considered driving crazy."

I had nothing. I stood, looking stupid yet equal before the law, waiting for a guilty verdict, a slight scolding, a small fine, and some court fees.

The old white judge sat up in his chair and glared at me as if he had just caught me in bed with his daughter.

With a voice so severe that he grabbed the attention of everyone in the courtroom, he snarled, "Mr. Davis, I find you guilty. Your driver's license is immediately suspended for six months. You will pay a fine of six hundred dollars plus court fees today, or you will spend six weeks in jail." He stood up, slammed the gavel down, and walked out.

The entire courtroom gasped. No one moved. The prosecutor was the first person to exhale. It took a few seconds before he then started shuffling his papers and putting them in his briefcase.

There was no way I could come up with six hundred dollars plus court fees by the end of the day. Was I really going to jail just for *speeding*? As I stood there, I noticed that I was not alone in my state of disbelief. People in the courtroom were murmuring. I got a blank glance from the patrolman. I couldn't believe this was happening.

For some reason, I thought that I should go to the patrolman for help. "Hey, officer, what just happened? I can't pay six hundred dollars. I can't go to jail for this. I have to go to school. I'll lose my car. I'll lose my apartment. I'll have a record. I won't be able to work."

The panic was setting in, and I was tearing up. "Is there anything you can do?"

The officer said, "I thought that was pretty harsh, but I can't do anything."

As we stood in the path of the prosecutor trying to leave the courtroom, I pleaded, "Can you ask him if there is anything he can do?"

"Who? The prosecutor?"

"Yes, please."

"Hey, Jim," the patrolman called to the prosecutor, "That was a pretty hard ruling. Do you think the judge would reconsider? He *is* a college student."

"I swear I was not driving recklessly. I don't know who called, but that caller was exaggerating, if not flat out lying," I explained.

"Can the judge lower the fine or give me more time to pay? I can't go to jail for six weeks." The prosecutor paused for a moment to gauge my sincerity.

"The judge has retired to his chambers. He is not going to want to come out. Hell, it may get worse."

149

"For what it's worth, I think he's a good kid, Jim," the patrolman urged.

Seeing my tears, the prosecutor retreated to the judge's chambers. After a few minutes, he came out with the judge, who appeared a little irritated but not angry. My clothes were soaked with perspiration.

"Mr. Davis, the prosecutor has asked me to reconsider my decision. Tell me why this prosecutor should risk my wrath for you," the judge demanded.

Ironically, I was standing before a judge who had made a decision similar to the one I made a long time ago. When I was a child, I determined that my friend Jeremy was more socially valuable to me than my friend Michelle. Although I like them both equally as friends, Jeremy's friendship would provide me with more opportunities for eating candy than Michelle's friendship.

Similarly, the white marine and I were both citizens objectively equal before the law. Legal equality is objective. Conversely, social equality is subjective. Just as you may value a friend's ability to show up on time over another friend's inability to, there is no injustice in having a preference for timeliness, because punctuality is something within a person's control.

An *unjust* level of social equality in a Racist Society results from the elevation or devaluation of a race or a member of a race within that society for something outside of his control. Being a member of a particular race is a permanent attribute outside of one's control. Furthermore, a *just* level of social equality in a free market society, for those who lack skills, positive

150

social values, and behaviors requires that life is harsher until these attributes can be obtained and recognized.

Being black in a racist society is a permanent disadvantage. But being black in a free market society without the skills, values, and behaviors that lead to success is not a permanent disadvantage. It is a condition that *can be* altered.

That is both the beauty and the deficiency of the progress made during the Civil Rights Era. It is beautiful that I was equal before the law. But to that judge, I was not socially equal to my fellow white citizen headed off to war. Social equality didn't cross my mind at that time, I only saw a racist old white judge. In my mind, I could only hear Tracy and Lacy swearing that all whites were racist. "He may be wearing a black robe, but there's a white KKK robe under it."

At that moment, I was on my proverbial knees, begging that God would move the judge's heart and not allow him to ruin my life. At the mercy of both God's will and the will of a judge who sat on a bench in the historically racist South, I pleaded my case.

"I was speeding, and it was stupid, but I was only trying to get my girlfriend to class. She attends NC A&T. I'm attending NCCU," I explained. "Well, technically I lost my financial aid but…"

He interrupted, "You have two weeks to come up with three hundred dollars, or you'll spend six days in jail. Your driver's license will still be suspended, but you can drive to work and back home if you have a job to go to. Now, get out of my courtroom and don't let me see you here again."

151

My social value and his subjective opinion of it must have gone up a few clicks, or he must have denounced his previous devotion to racial prejudice within the span of five minutes because my race, which is an objective fact, sure did not change.

My defense team—which included the white patrolman, a white prosecutor, and me—breathed a sigh of relief. We all thanked the judge as he left the courtroom. I thanked my defense team and shook their hands. Even though I had to pay the fine and court fees, I walked out of the courtroom feeling victorious. I would not become a statistic that day.

*

What a Day

Several weeks after dodging the bullet in court, I found myself out of work and behind on all of my bills. Desert Storm seemed to be the standard excuse for why I was not getting work. Life as a Durmite was getting rough. I was checking in with the Financial Aid Office every other day, hoping that a decision would be made in my favor. That way, I would have the money I needed for tuition the next semester. I was becoming nervous about my ability to pay my bills, particularly since paying that traffic fine took all of my money. I desperately needed some good news.

On a Wednesday morning, I was watching TV alone in my apartment when the phone rang at 11 AM. "Hello, Mr. Davis," said the voice on the phone. "You have entered your third month without payment on your truck.

152

I'm calling to notify you that if payment is not in our office by Friday, we will take action to repossess your truck."

This scared me to death. I had only three days to come up with a payment. The television in front of me became a blurred mess of images and background noise as I fruitlessly racked my brain for a stopgap solution.

At 12 PM, I received another call, this time from the apartment manager:

"You are two months behind on your rent, and we will start eviction procedures if you don't make a payment by Friday."

I stayed on the phone with the apartment manager in an attempt to clarify what options might be available. The manager made it crystal clear that there *were no* options, other than the full and timely payment of the rent by Friday. She said there was nothing more to discuss and hung up the phone.

My head was reeling, my heart was pounding, and I wanted to throw up. I was searching for some wild card, something within my control. Anything— anything at all—within my own power to right the ship.

Then I received another call: "Mr. Davis, this is Pam from the Financial Aid Office. I'm sorry, but your request for an exception has been denied. You will have to either pay your tuition next semester in cash or go to college in Michigan and bring your GPA up, and then reapply for financial aid. Just get your GPA above a 2.0."

I hung up the phone and started crying. I had lost everything. I would have to return to Detroit a failure. It was the worst day of my life.

I called Angie and told her I would be coming to see her the next day and then heading back to Detroit. When Dee got home, I told him the bad news. I said it was a temporary setback, and that I would be back. His eyes got watery. "Everyone says that they will come back," he choked out, "But they never do."

I sold all my furniture, and even my sound system, for gas to make it back to Detroit with some pocket change leftover for food. I left Durham a failure, owing one of my best friends half of the rent.

Chapter 7

Back in Detroit

Again, I found myself scanning the newspapers for work. Eventually, I felt okay enough about things to catch up with Keith and Kevin. They were right where I left them, like toys in an old toybox. Their company was the sole highlight of my miserable existence. Otherwise, I had no girlfriend, no freedom, no job, and no hopes for a promising future.

Luckily, I found a job opening for an assistant to a commercial roofing team. I spoke with the owner of the company, Mr. McDermott, and told him I was very interested and that I really needed a job. Although he liked what I had to say, he told me that I would need to interview with his foreman, Earl, and asked if I could make it to the job site that afternoon.

The job site was a small building in a town called Ferndale. It was just to the north of 8 Mile Road and 8 Mile Scoonie territory. Feeling like such a nobody for the past few weeks had left me with a pent-up desire to at least *look like* somebody. So I put on my interview suit with a freshly ironed white shirt, a necktie, and leather dress shoes. Of course, I was more than a little overdressed for an interview with a contractor. In fact, Earl initially mistook me for an administrator of the building.

When I arrived in the parking lot, the world's most stereotypical-looking roofer was walking towards me. He was a white guy in his forties with skinny legs, a beer belly, and a long beard. I asked if he was Earl, and somehow this man was able to spit tobacco and answer me at the same time. Earl chuckled when he realized I was the guy he was expecting for the interview.

"Normally I conduct the interviews on the roof, but I'd hate for you to get your suit dirty," he joked.

"I don't mind if I get dirty," I replied earnestly.

I climbed the ladder to the flat roof of the two-story building. Up there, I was introduced to the small crew of roofers. There was Samuel, an elderly black man with coal-black skin and two white men who looked to be in their forties, Phil and Ed. After explaining about the job and fielding a few questions from me, Earl joked that he was impressed that I managed not to fall off the ladder in my dress shoes. In spite of my suit, I got the job.

When I wasn't at work, I started to hang out with Kevin a lot. His criminal activities seemed to be returning astonishing profits. He was buying houses and fixing them up to either sell or rent. My return to Detroit was a blessing to Kevin because he was literally having explosive car problems: in fact, someone blew up his car in his driveway right after I left for school. The insurance company bought him a new one in a different color. Then, someone blew that car up. Now, he was in the process of fighting with the insurance company to convince them to give him another replacement after two such questionable "accidents."

He explained it all as if it were a minor nuisance. I asked Kevin if I should be concerned about being around him. After all, it was not the kind of news that inspired confidence. He smiled and said "No, the police had caught the guy. He was a jealous and slightly mental kid who lived around the corner."

Despite having a job and a social circle, the sting of being back in Detroit and sleeping under my parents' roof yet again awaited me every morning when I awoke. That is, until my uncle requested that I stay in one of his rental properties rent free while he got some renovations done to it.

I couldn't escape Detroit, but at least I would be able to escape my old bedroom and be on my own again in my "own" place.

Staying alone at my uncle's house afforded me a degree of freedom that could not be obtained living with my parents. My friends and I did not hesitate to take advantage of this, either. After a few weeks of living in my uncle's house and entertaining friends, it appeared that I would be living there quite a long time. Renovations were, indeed, moving slowly.

Before I knew what happened, the summer was here and with it came my Detroit friends from NCCU. It was great to see everyone, but I felt as though I was in prison and they were just coming for visitation. When Angie stopped by the house for what felt like a conjugal visit, I realized she was moving on in life and leaving me behind in Detroit. Our relationship would not last the summer.

*

KKK and the Former Slave

"Now the poor Ku Klux man say that we're all brothers
Not because things are the same but because we lack the same color
that's green,
now that's mean
Can't burn his cross cause he can't afford the gasoline."
-Lupe Fiasco, "American Terrorist."

Within a few weeks of working as a roofer's assistant, I began to feel like I was becoming part of the roofing crew. They had been together for years, and all knew one another very well. On that roof, they were all brothers and I was the visiting cousin. For the most part, I had nothing in common with any of them, but we all shared a pretty good sense of humor.

Phil and I were closest in age, but he was married with a kid. He loved heavy metal and Harley Davidson motorcycles. Phil was a redneck, plain and simple, and that is what everyone called him. He was quick-tempered and always yelling out complaints. Most of his yelling would be directed at Samuel. Likewise, Samuel would constantly yell at Phil.

157

The dynamic between Phil and Samuel was by far the most enjoyable part of my workday. They bickered all day, every day. Phil played the role of the strong-willed son who yells at his father for trying to do too much. Samuel played the role of the aging father trying to prove that he still had a thing or two to teach his son. They were like real-life incarnations of Lamont and Fred Sanford.

Samuel was by far the oldest of the crew by twenty or so years. He was as black as the tar we poured and as strong as a bull. He would display feats of strength so amazing that I felt like that old man could knock down a house with his bare hands. Samuel had eighteen kids from three marriages and seemed to be proud of every single one. Especially his youngest, who was six years old.

He treated me with more respect than I felt like I deserved. If I had trouble with any aspect of the job, he would be the first to offer to lend a hand or even take over. His demeanor when interacting with Earl, Ed and Mr. McDermott reminded me of the interactions you'd witness in old films whenever a slave hand would interact with a white person.

Let me be clear: Samuel was by no means undignified when interacting with white people. However, he definitely displayed a very subservient demeanor. Except, of course, when he dealt with Phil, the redneck.

One day towards the end of the summer, I complained to Phil that I had to get my truck's oil changed after work. Phil offered to change the oil himself for me at his house and save me some much needed cash. All I would need to do was to buy the oil and oil filter. I accepted his offer. However, because the city he lived in had a reputation amongst black Detroiters as being a highly racist city, I qualified my acceptance by jokingly asking for an escort in and out of Dearborn.

When I arrived at his house, he was standing on his porch with his wife and infant son. He waved me up the driveway and he and his family came to greet me. His wife was very nice and welcoming, but she and the baby retreated into the house rather quickly so that we could get to the business at hand.

Phil was working underneath my truck when we heard a motorcycle coming toward the house. The sound must have been distinctive because Phil shot out from under the truck before the motorcycle was even within sight. With no explanation, he told me to hide behind his garage and not to come out. I knew from the look in his eyes not to ask why. I immediately took cover as told.

Phil walked down the driveway to greet a visitor. I could not see who the visitor was, only that he was a white man of about Phil's age. From the casual air of the conversation, I could tell that they were good friends. The guy noticed my truck in the backyard and started asking questions while walking up the driveway.

"What are you doing with this thing, Phil?"

"I just brought it home to change the oil for a coworker," Phil explained.

"Huh?" the guy retorted.

Whether good or bad, people always commented on the appearance of the truck. But the visitor's concern was not the aesthetics of the truck. Instead, he sounded very concerned about the mere presence of the truck in Phil's backyard. Their conversation lasted about ten minutes, concluding with the visitor demanding that Phil get that truck the hell out of his backyard.

When the coast was clear, I walked out of hiding. I was vaguely frightened, though I couldn't quite pinpoint why.

"What was that about?" I asked.

"I went to high school with him," Phil said.

"So why did I have to hide behind the garage?"

"Because he is in the Klan."

"What?" I blurted out. "You have a friend in the Klan?"

He lightheartedly laughed and said, "technically. I'm in it too. But, obviously, not really."

Obviously? What the hell did that mean? When I tried to make a beeline to my truck, he implored me to calm down.

"Listen, we sell drugs from time to time. That's why he dropped by and why he was concerned about your drug dealer truck."

Wow! He was a Klansman selling drugs. I could not believe I lived in a world where I attended school with 7 Mile Black Killers and worked with a Klan member both of them selling drugs and taking pride in killing black people.

Phil unapologetically went on to explain his fair-weather-racist lifestyle.

"I have not dealt with the Klan in months, so there is no need to worry about it."

160

"Too late, Phil. I was worried when you told me to hide. Now I'm freaking out."

"The Klan thing was just something to do. I just have fun drinking and selling drugs. My relationship with you and Samuel should tell you without a doubt that I don't believe in the propaganda."

As I stood there listening to Phil, the constant mantras of Tracy and Lacy played in the background—all their goings on about how all white people were racist.

Phil took my silence as an indictment of his character. He felt a need to put some proof behind his words. He asked me to recall paydays and how we all would go to the corner store and cash our checks.

"Did you ever notice that Samuel and I are always at the register together?"

In all honesty, I hadn't noticed before. But I definitely remembered those two bickering at a register at one point or another. I thought nothing of it at the time. As he started to move me out of the way and position himself to finish the job under the truck, he continued on matter-of-factly, "Samuel is totally illiterate. The man can't read or even write his name. I sign his checks for him. If I'm not there, he takes it to his wife to sign it for him."

My shock of my friend being in the Klan was momentarily overshadowed by the surprise that someone could be illiterate in this day and age.

"So, you see, if I were a true believer, I'd let him and his family starve. But some of those guys have been my friends for years, so I just go through the motions. But don't worry, man, they are not the type of guys who run around lynching people."

Before this conversation, I had considered Phil to be a good friend. But now I felt like I needed to run for safety. I couldn't decide if I wanted to beat Phil up or just keep my mouth shut.

As he continued to try to reassure me, Phil finished up the oil change and invited me to stay for some beers. Even though our personal history should have been enough evidence for me to accept his offer, I politely turned down his invitation. Assuring him that despite this new revelation, things between us would be okay—hell, I had to work with the guy—I made up an excuse not to stay and left.

I worked with a member of the Klan and a great black guy named Samuel who often brought to mind the image of a recently emancipated slave. Needless to say, my conversation with Phil that day gave me new insight into his relationship with Samuel and the nuances of their friendship. After calming down as I drove home, I realized that Phil and I were both in somewhat of the same situation. We both had very influential groups of people in our lives telling us not to trust our fellow citizens and to even hate our fellow citizens based solely upon their race.

*

The Canadians

One night, as Keith and I drove through downtown Detroit, we decided we were both completely bored with all Detroit nightlife. We decided to go across the border and check out Windsor, Ontario. We had been to Canada with our families numerous times in the past and thought that maybe Canada's nightlife could offer us something fresh and exciting.

Keith had recently started wearing a beaver fur coat, and I had on a very expensive looking leather jacket. In short, in my truck and that clothing, no one would have mistaken us as two young men journeying into Canada to do missionary work. As we headed toward the tunnel to Canada, we grew concerned about our attire and what the glossy red truck so many local bangers envied might represent to white Canadian customs officers.

We approached the border looking like two drug dealers. Keith had recently purchased a radar detector that he brought with him even when he wasn't driving. I asked him if it was legal to have one in Canada. He said he did not know, but he would just hide it when we got there.

When you emerge from the tunnel, right away you notice Windsor's cleanliness relative to Detroit. You also notice the lack of black people relative to Detroit and how everyone seemed so nice and carefree. There was definitely more than a body of water separating Detroit from Windsor.

As we got close to the entrance of the tunnel that connects Detroit to Canada, we noticed a huge sign: "Radar detectors are not legal in Canada. Radar detectors found in vehicles entering Canada must be surrendered to Canadian border authorities."

"Keith, radar detectors are not legal in Canada," I said.

"That's okay, I'll just hide it under the seat. If we are not using it, what do they care?"

163

We pulled up to the checkpoint, and the Canadian customs officer immediately told us to pull over to the side for a random search of the automobile. Naturally, they found the radar detector.

"We have to confiscate this radar detector. There are signs posted in Detroit that state that radar detectors are illegal in Canada."

Ignoring what the officer just said, Keith, asked, "Could we just return to Detroit with the radar detector and come back to Canada some other day?"

The officer replied with an unemotional "No, in fact, not only do I have to confiscate the device, I have to issue you a fine."

The trip to Canada was starting out pretty badly. Keith was upset, but we decided to make the best of the evening and go pick up some girls. We made our way away from the Canadian border, turned the nearest corner, and were immediately signaled to pull over by a police officer in a patrol car. With the lights and sirens of the cop car came expletives from Keith that Canadians are just as racist as Americans.

I pulled over into a nearby McDonald's parking lot. Eventually, there were three patrol cars in my rearview mirror. My truck was surrounded by Windsor police officers. Soon, the McDonald's customers, who had left the restaurant to see what was going on in the parking lot, surrounded the officers.

"Do you know why I pulled you over?"

"No, sir."

"Your driver's side rear taillight is out."

"Oh, really?"

"Yes. Where are you guys headed?"

164

"I don't know. We were just going to check out the nightlife. No real plans."

"Are you visiting anyone?"

"No."

"Are you carrying anything you should not be carrying?"

"No, sir."

"Okay. I'll have to write you a ticket for the tail light infraction. Let me see your license and registration."

I handed over the requested materials. As he took a step toward his car, he hesitated and ambled back to my window.

"Do you mind if we look in your truck?"

"No problem. Go ahead," I responded. Keith and I stepped out of the truck and let the officer look inside the cab. After about a minute of looking, he popped his head out.

"Okay. I'll be right back with your ticket."

As he wrote the ticket, a pretty officer came up to me and started a conversation about how she liked my truck. She asked what type of sound system I had in it. For a minute, I forgot I was getting a ticket. I told her that I'd recently downgraded, but I was previously the proud owner of the world's greatest sound system. She showed genuine interest. Then, the other officer returned and told me the procedure to follow to take care of the ticket and to enjoy the rest of my stay in Windsor.

The patrol cars left the lot, and I got back into the truck. Keith was lingering outside on the passenger side. I yelled at him to get in the truck, so we could go home. He pointed out the crowd of interested and cute spectators that had not returned to the inside of McDonald's. Without a word, he closed the door and made his way across the lot to what looked like a group of journalists waiting for a story from an official at City Hall. I was in no mood to try and hit on any girls, so I hung back and watched Keith do his work.

I was not a good wingman that night. Eventually, Keith jogged back to the truck holding a piece of paper with a girl's phone number. He said that I was being rude and that I should at least say hello. So, as we drove off, I said hello and apologized to ten or so strangers, eight of which were women, for being anti-social. A few in the crowd were cute, and I instantly regretted my antisocial behavior.

A few weeks passed, and Keith came over to the house to announce that we had dates to see the Canadian girls. I had no idea what he was talking about. He explained that he had been calling one of those Canadian girls for the past few weeks and had arranged for us to go over and hang out with her and a friend.

"Which girl?" I asked.

"Does it matter? Do you remember seeing an ugly one?"

"No."

"So, let's go."

We jumped in my truck with our drug dealer uniforms on and headed back to Canada. When the Canadian customs officer asked the usual question of what our business was in Canada, this time we had a definitive answer.

"We're here for a visit," I announced.

166

"Who are you visiting?"

"Friends."

"What are your friends' names and where do they live?"

"Her name is Neina. I have her address right here."

"How long to do plan on staying here in Canada?"

"Oh, just a few hours."

The customs officer gave a friendly wink and said, "okay, have fun."

"I guess they are not all bad," Keith said as we pulled away.

We arrived at our destination. The only thing I knew about the girl I was going to see was that she was white and named Felicia. My impulse to discriminate could not outdo my instinct to procreate.

Although Keith attempted to jog my memory, I had no recollection of how Felicia looked. He claimed that she was a tall white girl with an asymmetrical haircut, but it wasn't ringing any bells. I resigned myself to just be there to support Keith in his carnal pursuit of the opposite sex. Anything I got out of it would just be a bonus."

We parked the truck and walked up to the door of a tall, well-kept apartment building of at least fifteen stories. We rang the doorbell and waited. Two other men promptly came up behind us, a bit too close for comfort, and rang another doorbell. Neina buzzed us in, and the two other guys followed us into the building and headed straight to the elevators.

As they got on the elevator, I mumbled to Keith, "Geez, Canadians didn't get the memo on personal space."

167

Neina quickly came around the corner and greeted us. She mentioned that Felicia was upstairs in their apartment and would be down shortly. She suggested that we all wait for her at their apartment manager's place, with whom they were good friends.

We followed her to the manager's apartment on the ground floor. The door of the apartment opened to a long corridor that branched out to the left for the kitchen and to the right for the living room, bedrooms, and outdoor patio.

We were introduced to the manager and her boyfriend, who were both white and about our age. There was also a very cute girl of Hawaiian descent. Keith reacquainted himself with everyone. I did not remember anyone, so everyone introduced themselves to me. After the formalities, we were quickly offered beer and weed, but we turned down both. Keith was trying his hand at professional boxing, so smoking and alcohol were off limits, while I just wanted to see how things played out before my mental state was altered.

As everyone passed around the joint, I inquired about Felicia. Neina apologized for her tardiness and called their apartment. When Felicia did not answer, Neina said that she must be on her way down. That was all right with me. We were having a good time anyway. After a little while, everyone smoked some cigarettes to get rid of the weed smell. I did not like the smoke, so I took a seat up against the wall between the living room and the kitchen, which directly faced the long corridor and front door.

Boom Boom Boom! There was a thunderous knock coming from the front door, and I knew that it was not friendly. Flashbacks of that night in the projects froze me in my chair. Although everyone heard the knock, it was mostly drowned out by the music to the people in the other room. I was the only one who realized how hard the door was being beaten. *Boom Boom Boom*!

"Windsor police!"

"Oh, hell no."

The manager of the apartment yelled, "Mike, quit all that banging! It's too late to be making all that noise!"

"This is the Windsor police. Open this door!"

Adrenaline was pumping through every vein in my body.

"I don't think that is Mike on the other side to the door," I shouted.

"Open the door, or we will knock it down!"

The manager turned the radio down.

"Mike, is that you?"

Boom! The door flew open, and I was staring down the barrels of five handguns drawn by five officers of the Windsor Police Department.

I yelled, "I don't think that this is Mike!"

The officers hollered, "Show me your hands!"

I put my hands up, and they rushed towards me. I was seized from my seat and thrown on the ground. Soon, just about everyone in the apartment was on the floor with me. We were all handcuffed. I could not believe what was happening. Keith was moaning about how he was going to explain getting thrown in jail in Canada to his mother. I looked over my shoulder to see the face of the officer with her knee on my back and realized it was the same pretty officer from the other day.

169

I told Keith to relax. We were not going to jail. We hadn't done anything wrong.

"Hey, I remember you from McDonald's," I said as cordially as I could manage with a knee pressed into my back. She remembered me as well and let up slightly.

"Oh yeah. Did you get that light fixed?"

"Yeah, I did. But what is this about?" She turned me over, stood me up, put me back in the chair and started to explain what was going on.

They were searching for a gun that belonged to an associate of that girl Felicia I was supposed to be seeing, which had been used in a shooting in Windsor a few weeks back. The officer in charge pulled out three glossy color mug shots, two of the girls we were there to see, and one of a black guy I had never seen before. The pretty officer ran down some crimes that these twin felons were guilty of.

While I was in handcuffs in the manager's apartment, my date was in handcuffs twelve floors above us. The two guys that had walked into the building with us had gone to the twelfth floor with a search warrant for Felicia's apartment. After their hunt for the gun had turned up fruitless, they asked her where they could find Neina. That is how Keith and I ended up on the floor in handcuffs with a bunch of strangers.

No gun was found in either apartment. Eventually, we were all released. "Enjoy the rest of your stay in Windsor," the officers said right before departing, as though they had not just initiated this traumatic encounter. Keith almost beat the police out of the apartment. He reminded me that every time we came to Windsor, we had endured some variation of being stopped, searched, having property confiscated, getting fined, and/or being put in handcuffs. He wanted to go home, and *fast*. Despite our dismal track record, I remained optimistic. The glossy color mug shot of my date had really appealed to me.

"No, dude. Let's make the most of this. Let's at least wait to meet Felicia," I said in an attempt to talk Keith down. Figuring things could not possibly go any further downhill, he agreed to wait a little while before returning to Detroit. Felicia came down, and what started out as a scary situation turned out to be a great night.

Keith and I wound up visiting our felonious Canadian friends over the next few months, and they visited us in kind in Detroit. But we eventually had to stop seeing the Canadians; the international phone bills and going through customs all the time started to be too much of a hassle.

During our relationship with the Canadian felons, I realized that their initial attraction to us was based on the assumption that we were criminals and "about that life." If Keith and I had been pulled over at the McDonald's in a plain Honda Accord, they would not have paid us any attention. Their dating history was filled with thugs from Detroit.

But perhaps what is sadder is that if the typical American saw the four of us together, and they were asked to choose the two felons in the group, we would have been the two they selected, of course.

I'm Just Doing This Right Now

My reign as regent over my uncle's castle had come to an end. The house had been sold. I had to bite the bullet and move back home. As if that wasn't bad enough, things got so slow at work that I was laid off. I was losing a paycheck and another new set of friends.

I managed to find a job at an oil change shop down the street from my parents' house called Oil Express. They were famous for quick oil changes and fluid checks in seven minutes or less. I recognized the manager as a guy from high school. I got to work with other young black men; some were fresh out of jail and on parole. Because all I did was talk about going back to NCCU, the guys started to call me "College."

We worked hard and laughed all day long about life, women, and black politics. The pay was horrible, but it was a decent job that paid the car note and allowed me to put gas in my truck.

The lack of privacy really put a cramp in my style as far as dating was concerned. There was nothing in the immediate future that told me my situation would change. I still owed money to NCCU so I would be stuck at home for the foreseeable future. The fact that my truck and style of dress made me appear as though I could take a girl back to my place for a nightcap, when I really couldn't, made life all the more frustrating.

Whenever I went out, I tried not to meet girls in the vicinity of my truck. Otherwise, I was stereotyped as a rich drug dealer from the second anyone saw me with it. I never got mad about it. After all, I chose to buy that particular truck. But it was just a pain to have to explain to the girl that although I appeared to have a lot of expendable cash due to illegal activities, I was actually broke and living at home.

A typical conversation would go as follows:

"Hi, how are you?"

"Fine. How are you?"

"I'm doing okay."

"So, what do you do?"

I would reply honestly. "I'm currently working at an oil change place."

She would then glance at the drug dealer truck before retorting, "Yeah, right."

Then I would smile and say, "I'm serious."

"Okay, but you don't look like you change oil."

"I am changing oil right now, but I'm trying to get back in college," I would explain.

The girl would then look at me as if I had said something unfathomable. A conversation about my future aspirations never lasted long.

One day, I got another "I need a ride" call from Keith. He needed me to chauffeur him to the Friday's on Evergreen Road and 11 Mile to meet a girl named Kim for dinner. Fridays was about two minutes from Keith's house by car, but thirty minutes from mine. I had no desire to hang out, mainly because I was trying my best to save money and getting nowhere fast.

Keith said the girl he was seeing had a friend, and that I would not be disappointed. One thing I gave Keith credit for is that although he never chipped in for gasoline, he usually had a blind date set up for me in advance. I was never relegated to being a third wheel. To be honest, every time

I had gone on a double date with Keith, his date would show up with a friend that looked better than the girl he was with. I thought that it would be worth the trip just to rub it in. And, since Keith did not tell Kim I was coming along, I had a way out if her friend was ugly.

I dressed in my best and drove thirty minutes to pick up Keith. From Keith's house, we drove two minutes to the restaurant. We saw Kim and her friend from afar in the restaurant parking lot. My winning streak was intact. Kim was light skinned and pretty, but Dagny was dark skinned and gorgeous, sporting a long ponytail.

"Damn!" Keith exclaimed.

I just laughed and said, "I guess I'll be staying."

We walked into Friday's together and sat at the bar. Kim informed us that she had five or six more girlfriends who were planning to show up. We reassured her the more, the better.

As Dagny and I got to know each other, I learned that she was two years older than me, living with her boyfriend, and attending Southern University in Louisiana. She had plans on attending law school at the University of Michigan after she graduated the following summer. The girl was perfect inside and out. Except, you know, for the boyfriend and living in Louisiana.

When it came time to tell my story, I figured I should just be as bluntly honest as possible and see what happens. I told my story of getting kicked out

174

of NCCU because I partied instead of studying. I explained that I had originally been in the pre-dental program, but lately, I was thinking that I would like to be a physician. I expounded on my struggles with financial aid and explained that although it looked as though I was selling drugs, I was actually changing oil at Oil Express.

I explained that despite really wanting to return to school in the South, I had recently settled for enrolling at the local community college. However, I wasn't able to come up with the nine hundred dollars I still owed NCCU. I felt like I was pouring out my soul to a psychiatrist.

She believed me when I said I was determined to leave Oil Express in the fall to be a full-time student. But I was not honest enough with her or myself to admit the fact that I would miss the fall enrollment because I had not saved nearly enough to pay off the nine hundred dollars, let alone pay for tuition. Despite all evidence to the contrary, my delusions were so strong that I convinced the both of us that I would follow through.

She seemed genuinely interested in my story of struggle, maybe even a little proud of me. We got along wonderfully. She encouraged me not to give up. She went on to say that based on the sincerity and determination in my voice, she truly expected me to be enrolled in the fall.

During our conversation, several of Kim's and Dagny's friends started to arrive at the restaurant. We all hit it off well and ended up hanging around well past midnight. When it came time to say goodbye, I told Dagny that I had had a blast with her but that out of respect for her relationship with her boyfriend, I would refrain from asking her for her telephone number. It may

175

have sounded chivalrous, but the fact of the matter was that I was living at my parents' home and could not even afford to buy her more than one drink. With that, we simply parted ways.

The next day, Keith informed me that Dagny wanted my phone number, so he had given it to Kim to pass along. The following day, I got a phone call from Dagny. We arranged for me to drop by her house, which was about ten minutes away from my parents' house. At her home, we talked and had a good time, and then set up a date to go out. The date never happened. I told myself that she was probably not prepared to jeopardize her relationship with her boyfriend.

Life went on with me working at Oil Express and trying, but failing, to pay off my debt to NCCU. When autumn rolled around, I could not enroll in community college. Then the new year came, and I missed yet another enrollment deadline.

Life went on like this until I went to work in a blizzard one day in February. Due to the weather, the shop was very slow. The fellas and I spent the day telling jokes and talking about girls and politics as usual. Towards the end of the day, I decided to clean up the basement of the shop. I was yelling jokes upstairs, and they were yelling stuff downstairs. Then, as though someone had pushed a mute button, all of the guys upstairs suddenly went quiet. With rather excessive geniality, I heard Ray, the manager, cut through the silence and say, "Welcome to Oil Express. May I help you?"

I went about my business to prepare to work on the customer's car. But instead of shouting the usual "car coming around," Ray dashed down the steps with a huge smile on his face.

"College, there is a fine-ass woman upstairs asking for you."

"Really?"

"Oh yeah."

I knew she was fine by how quiet the fellas upstairs were. As I reached the top of the stairs, I could see a dark-skinned black woman with a ponytail. She was wearing a long cashmere coat and looked ravishing. It was Dagny. I walked up to her, proud that such a beautiful girl stopped by to see me in the middle of a blizzard. I knew I would be considered the man at the shop for this. I would be a legend.

I was so happy to see her but, as I approached, I noticed that she had a blank expression on her face. She didn't really seem happy to see me, nor did she appear to have any car problems.

She stood in a spot that was sonically secluded from the rest of the shop. We were visible to everyone, but no one could hear our conversation.

"Hi, Dagny. It's so good to see you!"

"I saw the truck and the Oil Express sign, and said, 'I wonder if that is Andre's truck.'"

I smiled and replied, "Yep, that's my truck."

With a hint of disappointment, she said, "I see you're still working here."

With that little kid from the projects smile, I replied, "Yep, all day, every day."

She seemed hesitant to utter a follow-up question or statement. She was waiting to hear more, but I had nothing more.

Breaking the increasingly awkward silence, I uttered, "Just here working." I wasn't smiling anymore.

Her eyes narrowed. "What the fuck are you still doing here? I thought you were going back to school," she rebuked. Her voice cut through me like a light saber.

My smile withered. No one, not even my parents, had ever looked at me with such palpable disappointment. I stood there speechless, feeling like a jackass. The only thing I could do was to spit out excuse after excuse about why I was still working at Oil Express and had not re-enrolled. Then, I realized that she had stopped listening. She was not there to hear my excuses.

"I wasn't lying to you. I have been trying to get back in school all this time. I didn't plan for it to take so long. I need you to believe what I'm telling you."

"Well, Andre, I don't think you were lying. You just are not trying hard enough. After all of this time, I expected a lot more out of you than to just be working here."

"Well, I'm technically the assistant manager," I replied, hoping for some validation.

She rolled her eyes and responded impatiently, "So?"

I felt so small. Small enough that I could jump off a street curb and the fall would do me in. I tried to change the subject by asking what she was up to. She briefly mentioned that she was doing an internship at General Motors, and I congratulated her.

Then, she abruptly ended our encounter. "Well, Andre, good luck."

She walked out. I turned towards the crowd of co-workers who had gathered at the back of the shop. As soon as the door closed, they all ran towards me to ask about her. I told them that she was the girl of my dreams that I had told them about during so many of our talks. I also told them what she said. They said they felt my pain.

At that, I raised my head, stuck out my chest, and declared, "I'm getting out of the oil-changing business and going back to school."

If she had not asked me that question—what the fuck I was still doing at Oil Express—in that manner, you would not be reading these pages. She did not know it, but Dagny gave me a gift that day.

Dagny held me to a higher standard than anyone else ever had. Her expectations of me were higher than anyone else's, including my own. I never looked in the mirror and asked myself that question in that manner. Neither did my parents, long-time friends, members of our church, or society at large.

With all of the horrible statistics that get trumpeted about rates of death and incarceration for black males, it's easy to have low expectations for a young black man from Detroit. To many, just staying out of trouble was an accomplishment for someone like me. My own family celebrated that I had made it to my eighteenth birthday with neither an illegitimate child or criminal

179

record. That person may be winning in a racist society, but he isn't winning in a free market society.

Unlike my family, my friends, and the media, Dagny didn't accept the premise that I was winning just because I had survived. Furthermore, up until that time, I had bought into another common narrative that incredibly beautiful women reserved their attention for sporty guys with the potential earning capacity of a professional athlete, or otherwise drug dealers that had immediate buying power. But that was not the case with Dagny. She saw the potential I had based on my ambition and intellect, rather than on the color of my skin.

*

On a Mission

I dedicated myself to returning to school by the fall of 1994. My drive to succeed had been pushed to a level that was unimaginable just the day before. My focus was laser-precise. I swore to myself that I would do everything I could to clear my debt and pay cash for four classes at Oakland Community College.

I stopped hanging out with my friends and wouldn't go on any dates of any kind. Coincidentally, Keith helped me get a second job as a merchandiser with him for 7-Up.

When the fall semester rolled around, I had paid off my debt to NCCU and had enough cash to pay for twelve credits' worth of classes at Oakland Community College. The boost to my confidence was enormous. I had seized the control that had eluded me for so long. I was taking twelve credits four

180

nights a week and working two jobs during the day. I was in a perpetual state of exhaustion, but it was the happiest, most fulfilling time of my life.

By the time midterms rolled around, I had established myself as the smartest person in all of my classes. I was as focused as I had ever been in school, even more so than when I told my mother I would make the honor roll if she agreed to buy me a scooter. People that knew me said that I had changed. Those who did not know me told me that I had an air of urgency. The lowest grade that I had received by the middle of the semester was a ninety-six percent. Everything else was one hundred percent or more.

Academically, everything was going great. Socially, I did not exist, and economically, I was hurting. My job at 7-Up was slowing down, so I was not working as many hours. Paying off my debt to NCCU and paying cash for my 12 college credits put me two months behind on my car note. But I did not care. The only thing I cared about was getting back into a four-year institution.

To do that I would need to offset the previous twenty-four credits with a combined GPA of 1.71 with the twelve credits I was currently earning. My overall GPA would have to be at least a 2.0 to qualify for financial aid. However, I did not know what GPA I would need to be admitted to a four-year institution, so I planned to combine twelve credits of straight A's with twenty-four credits of all D's and pray.

Although my friends and family said that I had changed, my race never did. It was my priorities and values that had shifted. So much so that when the finance company that held the loan on my truck called again to tell me they were coming to repossess my truck, I didn't allow myself to be a victim of

181

circumstance. Instead, I called my friend Marco's father, an attorney, for bankruptcy advice.

I told him about my situation and that I just wanted to go to school to be a doctor. He told me not to file bankruptcy unless I would end up owing GMAC more than ten thousand dollars. He went on to tell me that he believed that government loans should be available to me regardless of my credit score, and that as long as I could find an institution with tuition that can be covered by academic scholarships and federal student loans, I should stay in school for the next seven or eight years and become a doctor.

By the time I became a doctor, he promised, the repossession would be off of my credit report. He finally cautioned that he was not giving me legal advice and that before I made any permanent decisions, I should verify that I would be eligible for federal student aid with repossession of the truck on my credit report.

I thanked him for his advice and hung up the phone. I immediately called the financial aid office at Eastern Michigan University. I was able to confirm that having bad credit would not affect my ability to qualify for federal student loans. Around 10:30 in the morning, the repo man showed up at my door, and I happily handed over the keys to a big part of my black identity.

I no longer wanted to project the image of a successful drug dealer. I just wanted to be a broke college student. In fact, I was proud to be one. They could take my truck away, but they could not take away my intellect and what it could accomplish.

Although I could walk to Oil Express, the lack of a vehicle left me without transportation to my classes. I researched bus routes to Oakland Community College and happily accepted taking two buses to school during Detroit's brutal winter. However, my enthusiasm turned to concern when I realized that there were no buses to take coming home.

One option was to ask my parents to drive out to the suburbs after they had been at work all day and pick me up from school, but I did not feel right about asking them to do that. It was my fault that I was in the situation, and I wanted to bear the consequences.

My first day of school with neither a car nor a care arrived with a snowstorm. I had to wait to see if the buses would even run. Luckily, they did, and I blissfully headed off to school with no worry about how I would get home.

I barely socialized, so I did not know a lot of people, but I asked a few classmates if they could give me a ride home or at least to somewhere near a Detroit bus route. After asking several people to no avail, I decided to take the challenge and walk home. That night I walked through the cold, snowy suburbs for eight and a half miles. When I arrived at my house, my parents assumed that I just caught the bus back home. I went upstairs to my room and went to sleep feeling invincible. I would continue to walk in the freezing cold from school without a care, and without my parents' knowledge, for the rest of the semester.

As finals neared, I realized that I was the teacher's pet in all of my classes. What a contrast from Hampton Middle School! I was feeling good about my chances of getting into Eastern Michigan University, so I sent in an application.

My only problem was getting my final grades to Eastern Michigan's registration office in time for them to decide whether I could matriculate into EMU for the winter semester. My final exams and the last day to have my complete application for admission for EMU were only a few days apart. I would need to rush all of my teachers to give me a final grade, get those grades to the OCC registrar's office, and then get my official transcripts to EMU.

Reaching that goal would have been impossible without a ton of help. My teachers, all of whom but one were white, graded my exams first and sent the grades to OCC registrar. The registrar, who was also white, gave me an office copy of my transcripts in a sealed envelope. I got a ride from Keith up to EMU and handed my transcripts over to a white administrator I had been in contact with concerning my application. As she promised, I saw her put my application on top of the other pile of applications that she had to consider.

Without the help of a single black social activist or the interference of a single Ku Klux Klan member, I matriculated to EMU with a financial aid package waiting for me.

*

Okay, One More Time

Eastern Michigan University's Ypsilanti may not have been the black cocoon of Durham, North Carolina, but it beat Detroit. Ypsilanti was safe, and I was surrounded by people going places and doing positive things. The girls were not as friendly as the girls from North Carolina, but I was not concerned with girls this time around. I had to make the best of my second chance.

I had a cool roommate named David. He was a black kid who lived near my grandmother back in Detroit. In general, I was surprised by the paucity of minority students on campus. Though my black identity told me that I should be concerned about this, I was I was more concerned with the fact that I was behind.

I always seemed to be the oldest guy in my classes. People with whom I had graduated high school would be graduating from college soon. Yet, there I was, still a freshman. I was even struggling with algebra. I had to take remedial algebra as a refresher course, but it was hard to refresh something that I had never properly learned in the first place. So I got a tutor but still struggled with that particular class.

I regretted the time I wasted in junior high when I was first exposed to the subject, and my struggles with algebra led me to change my mind about becoming a doctor. Instead, I wanted to be an attorney.

Outside of math, I was getting good grades despite my challenging course load. By my first midterm, I had established myself as a smart guy. People wanted me in their study groups. This must be what it feels like to be a six-foot nine-inch black guy on a basketball court in a non-black community. It was a complete role reversal compared to my first stint in college.

I was so grateful to be there and could not understand why anyone would not feel the same way. Once the honeymoon phase of being a college student wore off for many students, they would start complaining about how homework and quizzes were interfering with their social life. With an old, wise man's persona, I would remind them not to squander the opportunity at hand. Homework was just a reminder of what I had accomplished and the possibilities to come. Everything inside and outside of the classroom was suddenly interesting to me. I had a new appreciation for everything—and my future seemed as bright as ever.

Meanwhile, I was encountering several reminders of my past. An interesting string of events happened to me on back-to-back days as I walked along the same path on campus.

The first day, a black guy came up to me and said, "Hey, your name is Andre, right?"

I had no idea who the guy was, but figured he was in one of my classes. "Yes, I'm Andre," I replied.

"Do you remember me?"

"Should I?"

"Yeah. We went to DoReMe together."

"What? Dude, I went to DoReMe for one semester in the second grade."

"Yeah, man. I remember you."

"Wow!" I exclaimed.

His name was Ray Golden. After wracking my brain for a split second, I remembered him, too. We started off our friendship in 1994 from where it left off in 1976.

Coincidentally, the next day the same thing happened again, but in reverse. I was the one asking Noel Schulman, my super smart friend from Hampton Elementary, if he remembered me. It took him a second, but, with a smile, he said that he did. As we walked and tried to catch up on the time we'd lost, I made a bit of a fool of myself when I asked him what he was doing on EMU's campus. I never thought that my Ivy League-bound friend from Hampton Elementary would be enrolled at EMU with me.

"Oh," he answered, "I'm just heading home."

"Oh, you were visiting someone here?"

"Yeah."

The prestigious University of Michigan in Ann Arbor was only about fifteen minutes from EMU; I assumed that he meant he was enrolled there.

"Are you a student at U of M?" I asked.

"Nah, I go here."

"You go here?" I was shocked. "Man, I thought you would be at U of M, Harvard, or Yale. What happened?"

Noel was looking at me like I was nuts.

"What do you mean, 'what happened?'"

It occurred to me that I could have expressed myself a bit more diplomatically.

Just because Noel was white and had been smart in elementary school, I assumed that was enough to ensure a life free of struggle or strife. Life was supposed to be handed to him on a silver platter because he was a white guy in a racist society. However, life happened to Noel regardless of race.

187

Soon after his family left Detroit for the suburbs, he lost his father due to a sudden heart attack. Noel took the loss very hard. He went from being a studious, well-mannered kid to a troubled teen. He finally got his act together, and, according to him, barely got into EMU.

I had lost touch with two good friends. I was a bit saddened that, like so many of my old friends, I missed out on being part of their personal childhood experiences. But the usual narrative filled in a lot of the blanks. Although I had not seen Ray since the second grade, and he was just as smart as Noel, and I were, I had no difficulty with the reality that he was an EMU student. Conversely, I couldn't even imagine that Noel was at the same school with us.

By the end of my first semester, I knew that I would make the honor roll. But I wanted to do *something special now.*

I believed that studying abroad would be perfect for my future résumé, and thought that my good grades would help me get into a program in a non-English-speaking country. However, as I looked into various study abroad programs, it became clear to me that only rich people who could afford the tuition could take advantage of those opportunities. That, or geniuses who could qualify for scholarships. In some cases, a single semester abroad could cost as much as four years of tuition at EMU.

Although the initial sticker-shock was disheartening, I kept the idea in the back of my mind and decided that I'd get involved in some extracurricular activities in the meantime. I became a member of the Walton International Residence Hall Government, which was basically the student council of the dorm I was staying in. I attended dorm meetings where snacks were provided, and everyone complained about the lack of amenities in the dorm's cafeteria. With my future résumé in mind, I decided to major in political science, and, aptly, run for the presidency of Walton Hall for the upcoming fall semester.

*

Life as the President

One of the perks of the post was to be able to live in the president's dorm room, which included a living room that could double as a second bedroom. The dorm also boasted a kitchenette and a full bathroom. Plus, if I got a roommate, I would not have to pay for housing. It did not escape my notice that most students in the dorm were oblivious to the opportunity. Auspiciously, I ran uncontested.

As the semester moved on beyond midterms, I thought that life on campus was getting better and better. I was thoroughly enjoying my classes as the resident smart guy. In the dorm, the word was getting out that I would be the new president in the fall. The duties of the resident hall president began during the winter semester with an orientation meeting with newly elected presidents and returning presidents. At the orientation, I was happily congratulated and greeted by school faculty and the other presidents.

The only thing that I could ascertain about the other presidents was that they were white young adults with bright smiles and an interest in residence hall politics. I was the only non-white residence hall president on campus, but that did not stop me from making friends with a few of the other residence hall

189

presidents early on. It felt great to be rubbing elbows with the best and brightest of EMU's student body.

However, as I got to know my new friends, I was surprised to find out several of them were on academic probation. I'd assumed that these white kids were well-to-do, smart, and beyond reproach, but I was wrong. They were just as academically irresponsible as I had been at NCCU, and, just like me, saw being a residence hall president as an avenue towards redemption.

By the end of the semester, I was truly walking on air. I had accomplished everything that I wanted to scholastically. I had made a ton of great friends and had a fantastic roommate; I was the president of a dorm and the founder of a new social group. A social group that primarily ate pizza listen to music, and discussed the woes of black America with other black residents of the dorm. Besides general complaints about life in America for the black man, I had no specific complaints about my life except for two things: the inability to find an affordable study abroad program and learning that my roommate David would not be my roommate in the fall. As I signed up for summer semester classes, David decided that the college life was not for him and signed up for the Air Force.

Along with doing well during the summer semester, I prioritized finding a roommate for the fall. I had formed a pretty good relationship with the people in the housing department and, eventually, I was allowed access to the roster of students moving into Walton Hall in the fall.

I noticed someone whose address was about a block away from my cousin Kevin's address. I thought that there was a ninety-nine percent chance

190

that this guy named Mark Johnson was black, and that I knew him or at least knew someone who did. I decided to call him up.

An answering machine intercepted the call, and I was greeted by a man's voice. "Moshi moshi. Watashi no namae wa Maku desu. Tadaima rusu shiteimasu. Messeji o nokoshite kudasai" What in the hell? I muttered to myself. I almost hung up the phone right then. In a split second, he followed up in English, "Hello. This is Mark. I am not here right now, so please leave a message." I stood there holding the phone, not knowing what to think.

Frankly, I was stumped. Whatever the language was, it did not sound like Chinese, French, Italian, or German. It definitely was not Spanish. I thought that it was just my luck that I would find the only foreigner living in the University District. I almost hung up the phone without leaving a message.

But then I thought that I should leave a message just in case. I stated who I was and why I was calling. Still skeptical that I had reached the right guy, I stated emphatically, "I would appreciate it if Mark Johnson would call me back," and hung up the phone.

I did not receive a call that day or the next day. I decided to give Mark another day to call before I began a new search. The following day, I finally received a call from him. We spent the first few minutes trying to figure out if we knew each other. Though we concluded that we had never met before, we did have a friend in common. Like me, Mark often played basketball in my friend Eric's backyard. He knew of my cousin Kevin because his brothers and Kevin hung out together. It was odd that we had never met.

I got around to asking the pertinent question. "What language were you speaking on your answering machine?"

"Japanese."

"Wow! Where did you learn Japanese?"

Mark went on to tell me about a little-known work-study program that afforded students the opportunity to work and take college courses while living in Japan from January through December. It was called the "Japan Adventure." It was offered by Lansing Community College, and a railroad company in Japan called Keihan Electric Railway. The students would work as waiters on a Mississippi River boat called "The Michigan," which sailed around Lake Biwa in the prefecture of Shiga. Or they would go to the other site on the island of Shikoku, where the program was known as "New Horizon." Students there worked as waiters at what could best be described as a pseudo-amusement park modeled after San Francisco's Fisherman's Wharf called Keihan Fisherman's Wharf.

During the program, American teachers taught typical college classes such as political science and sociology with an emphasis on Japan. Japanese language classes were taught by native Japanese teachers. Rather than lousy dorm rooms, the students lived in their own apartments and toured Japan on the railroad company's dime. Students were also paid an excellent wage for their labor.

There was even a free three-day trip to South Korea, with hotel accommodations and tours included, at the outset of the program before arriving in Japan and a three-day vacation in Hawaii at the end of the program.

192

To top it all off, most of the students came back from the program with money in their pocket.

"This is too good to be true," I responded after Mark finished explaining.

"No, it's true. Why don't you apply?"

"I believe I most definitely will."

I was so excited about this opportunity that I nearly forgot about asking him to be my roommate. When I did, he agreed without hesitation. After just one conversation, I had a new roommate and a new opportunity.

After Mark and I had moved in together in the fall, I sent off my application for the program. Mark decided to apply to return to the program as well, but this time as a supervisor.

My new roommate was three years my junior, but a true Youngblood at heart. He was a Stevie Wonder *nut*. Every time I wandered into our presidential suite, Mark was belting out along with a different Stevie Wonder song. I was sharing a room with a black guy from my old neighborhood in Detroit who was fluent in Japanese. It was surreal.

In addition to our fondness of R&B and hip-hop music, we shared an interest in politics and social issues. Mark became my treasurer for Walton Hall and participated in my other student group. We were two conscious brothers kicking ass in class and having a responsible amount of fun in our off hours. We were aware of both the need for marketable skills and of our shared black identity.

Sadly, these two things often had us conflicted. We were respected on campus for academic acumen by our peers, but our disposition towards life and its possibilities put our focus outside of our black cocoon. Too many of our fellow black students, we were becoming "them." This has been particularly true for Mark due to his fluency in Japanese, coupled with the fact that he often took things like his residency in Detroit, Ypsilanti, or Japan for granted. While many of our peers would not consider residing outside of a predominately black community as an option, Mark often spoke of residency as if it were as simple as choosing a Stevie Wonder album.

*

Tracy, Lacy, and Lea

The day that Mark and I were both notified of our acceptance to the program was one of the happiest days of my life. I was excited and scared at the same time. Once again, I was going around telling people I was leaving, but this time due to a massive accomplishment and not a huge failure.

My desire to share my excitement about going to Japan fueled my motivation to find some of my old friends that I had lost contact with. Just like Noel, I had totally lost touch with nearly all of my friends who left the University District. I had not seen or heard from Tracy, Lacy or Juan for years. It took a lot of detective work, but I was able to locate Juan living on his own in a terrible neighborhood on Detroit's East Side.

I wanted to surprise him. So, I just showed up to his front door and rang the bell.

194

"Who is it?"

"It's Andre."

With a slight hint of recognition in his voice, he replied, "Andre?" A disheveled Juan opened the door. He looked like he had aged forty years. That sneaky grin had been replaced with a look of despair and hopelessness. However, when his eyes focused in and he began to remember who I was, whatever was causing the sad look on his face was erased instantly.

"Andre!"

The last time we saw each other, we were both in high school, and his outlook on life was just as positive and innocent as mine. We hugged, and he invited me into what could best be described as a pigsty. In spite of that, I felt like we would pick up right where we had left off.

Soon, I realized that I was talking to a father who had been married and divorced. He complained about barely being able to take care of himself, let alone his son, who was with Juan's mother at the time. That energetic Peruvian kid that I had met years ago, my brother from another mother, was nearly unrecognizable, both physically and emotionally.

Life was kicking his ass. I could tell that our brief reunion was a ray of sunshine cutting through his otherwise dismal existence.

He disclosed that his parents were doing well, but that he had just recently lost his grandmother. Our old conversations usually consisted of Juan talking ninety percent of the time. Things had not changed. After I listened to him paint a picture of his life of gloom and doom, he got around to asking if I had heard what happened to Tracy and Lacy.

195

His straightforward inflection prepared me for more bad news. Perhaps a similar story of woe, with a possible gunshot wound or some time spent in jail.

"No. What happened?"

"Tracy is dead, and I don't know what the hell happened to Lacy."

I sat frozen. Juan let the sentence drill into my head for a moment before saying, "yup, he got hooked on drugs and set himself on fire when his mother wouldn't give him more money so that he could buy more." Still frozen, I continued to listen.

"I'm surprised you didn't hear about it. It was actually in the news. You remember that they were selling that shit, but for some reason, Tracy got hooked, and Lacy didn't. Well, maybe Lacy did, but I never heard that he did."

"What happened to Lacy?"

"He's dead, or he skipped town, maybe. No one knows."

This type of bad news was common in Detroit. But, these were my friends. They had been guys who I looked up to. Guys who could have been contributing members of society, even if that society was a black cocoon. They were turned into statistics just like that.

Eventually, the conversation flowed to what I had been up to all this time. After all of that bad news—which I could tell by the way it was delivered was just plain-old-news to Juan, I downplayed everything. I didn't need to be over here bragging about my new, more hopeful life, my successes, or Japan.

With a hint of artificial annoyance in my voice, I said, "Man, I'm up at Eastern Michigan trying to graduate. It's been a long road, but hopefully, I'll be

196

done soon. I had to take some time off here and there and couldn't go straight through, but I'm trying."

"Well, keep trying, bro. Speaking of college, guess who I bumped into a few months back? You remember Lea from Hampton Elementary, right?"

Oh shit. I prepared myself for even more bad news.

"Of course," I said. "She was kind of my first real crush."

"It was crazy because I had not seen her since elementary school but recognized her right away. Man, she is fine as hell! I was downtown with my son when I ran into her and her son."

I was so eager to hear more that I blurted out, "Well, how is she doing?"

"She is fine. Hell, she is doing better than most. She said she was in college and about to graduate."

"Really? Damn! She had a kid before I had a mustache and she will graduate from college before me. Well, I ain't mad at her."

Grateful for some good news, we continued to catch up, and he asked about the Cubics. I told him that I had not seen the kids because they all had left the nest, but the parents were still there.

Coincidentally, the Cubics had become what Michelle's family was in the Brewster projects: the rare white family in a predominately black neighborhood.

Pretty soon, the time came for Juan to get ready for one of his part-time gigs as a security guard at a drug store. So, we parted ways. I was heartbroken about Tracy and Lacy, but I could not help but feel extremely proud of Lea.

197

Juan was the only person that I didn't tell about my opportunity to live and study in Japan too. When I did tell people that I would be living and studying in Japan for a year, they seemed very happy for me. However, many were confused as to why I would want to go to Japan. After all, the motor city had been losing jobs to Japanese automakers for about a generation, and our black cocoon was suspicious.

When I shared the news with my cousin Kevin, he sternly admonished, "Why are you going to Japan? Don't you know they don't like black people?"

To his credit, he had recently heard that the Japanese Prime Minister, Yasuhiro Nakasone, insulted black people by saying that our intelligence level was inferior, though he did later apologize for having his words misunderstood. I didn't care. This was an opportunity of a lifetime, and no prime minister or black identity was going to keep me from taking advantage of it.

Part III

Chapter 8

Japan here I come

The fall semester ended as quickly as it started. I was on my way to a bright future in Japan. However, I would first need to relocate to Lansing, Michigan for a crash course in what to expect while living and working in Japan. The program required that all of the student participants start our classes for that semester on Lansing Community College's campus. Then, in March, all of the participants, including our teachers, would relocate to Japan.

I was selected for the New Horizon program, which meant that I relocate to Sakaide City in Kagawa Prefecture. Meanwhile, Mark was on the Japan Adventure program and would be residing in Otsu City, Shiga Prefecture. We were all told that Sakaide was considered the countryside, while Otsu was found to be more urban. Both areas had their unique charm.

A few days before beginning regular classes in Lansing, I attended a special dinner to meet all of the members of both programs, including the teachers, student supervisors, sponsors, and many former participants. My New Horizon group included a supervisor named Theo who, like Mark, had been part of the program as a student the year before, and a girl named Pam, who had attended two years before.

I had an opportunity to meet all of my classmates as well. There was Anastasia, who was very outgoing and let everyone know that she was fun to

199

be around. Augustus could have been the protagonist in any movie about a fraternity. Bella was our resident Greek and middle child. Wendy was the tall all-American girl. Hugh was the shy kid who would eventually be responsible for most of the pranks that went on. Kyle was the suburban white boy from Bay City, Michigan. Kayla seemed to be a fashionista. She was half-white and half-Japanese. Margo was the redhead with long, flowing locks who was serious about most serious subjects. Jax was the wild card, a white guy with a rocker appearance. He was kind of a loner.

While at LCC, all of the participants stuck together. This was mainly because we were so excited about going to school that other students found our joy for attending classes irritating. While in Japanese class, we learned not only the language but also about Japanese customs and culture and what we could expect as we did our jobs as waiters.

I thought that Mark was joking when he told me if I was accepted, the program threw the participants into the fire immediately. But he wasn't lying at all. Within a week of arriving in Japan, with next to no Japanese language skills, I would be working as a waiter.

The program may have had a lot of faith in our abilities, but they took next to nothing for granted. They taught us how to set a formal dining table and utilize the utensils. This was necessary, as we would be dining with very important people, such as the mayor of the city and the governor of the prefecture. In addition to those heavy hitters, we would also be dining with prominent members of the Japanese economic community, such as the president of the Keihan Electric Railway. With this in mind, there was also a

200

formal lesson on how to use chopsticks. The program ran at breakneck speed; we were expected to absorb an impossible amount of information before departed from for Japan in March.

Whenever I did have a second to catch my breath, I just found it unbelievable that this kid from the Brewster projects would be wining and dining with Japanese captains of industry, mayors, and governors.

Before I knew it, the day came to say goodbye to friends and family and leave the United States. At the airport, we met some of the administrators. Dr. Tai Sung Kim was the co-founder of the program, as was the late Mr. Megumi Shigematsu. Dr. Kim was Korean, but he had studied in Japan, where he became college buddies with his co-founder. Together, they created the program about ten years before I participated. Fittingly, Dr. Kim wanted to showcase his home country of Korea, which was totally fine with all of us.

At that point, Korea was just as good as Japan. Both were foreign and Asian, and I knew next to nothing about either country. The participants of both the Horizon and Adventure programs boarded a plane in Detroit headed to JFK for a brief layover. Then we boarded Korean Air, bound for Seoul, South Korea.

We were so excited that we could not sit still. Everything that day seemed amplified. The trip to the airport felt extra short, the ticket line wasn't so long, but the wait to board that plane seemed like an eternity. Finally, we boarded the plane, sat down, and gave our full attention to the incredibly beautiful flight attendant, who was reading those same old instructions about what to do in an emergency.

As we settled down, I came to realize that on international flights, alcohol was poured freely and often. But something else was raising my eyebrows: Korean Air's flight crew—which was comprised of women so beautiful it was almost intimidating.

Of course, all of the guys noticed immediately. But it was Kayla who was the first to verbalize what we were all thinking. She wondered aloud, "Where did they get all of these models from?" I had never seen anything like it. I overheard Dr. Kim's lighthearted explanation that discrimination laws in Korea were not as progressive as they were in the United States. Korean Air only hired former Miss Korea pageant winners.

Not knowing or caring if that was true, I just enjoyed the ride. There I was: a kid from the projects being pampered by several women, any of who could have won a Miss Korea contest. Mark had a saying: "Life is great, and things are only getting better." I was overcome by the same sentiment.

We landed in Seoul, cruised through customs, and headed straight to our hotel under the abundance of neon signs lighting up Seoul's night sky. We were all eager to get some sleep to recuperate from the long trip and start our adventure in Seoul the next morning.

With the morning came our new tour guide, who was a childhood friend of Dr. Kim's. We were shown the Olympic stadium and visited a few factories. We went through several neighborhoods and were shown a bridge that had collapsed without warning. We saw the good, the bad, and the ugly, but we appreciated it all. We were met everywhere by people with smiles and varying degrees of English proficiency.

On the last day of the trip, we were taken to a place called Lotte World. It was an indoor amusement park. I wondered, who had thought of putting Disneyland inside a building? It had a full-size roller coaster, a plethora of other rides, an ice skating rink, and plentiful restaurants. As we marveled at the theme park's many attractions, we started to notice an unusual number of women in wedding dresses. And if they were not wearing a wedding dress, at a minimum, their faces were made up as if they were in a wedding. I don't know if it was the date or the place, but there were a lot of people getting married at the theme park that day.

We tried our best to interact with the girls at Lotte World with hand gestures, shoulder shrugs, and cheesy smiles. We enjoyed a one hundred percent success rate with making the girls smile, giggle, and then run off.

Everyone there seemed pretty indifferent to our presence, unless we tried to engage in some form of communication. But every once in a while, I noticed little kids alerting their parents to our presence by pointing at us and saying something in Korean.

To some degree or another, we were all concerned about our reception in a foreign land with an American military presence. However, there was another level of concern about my presence in Korea: my black identity.

Being an American minority, I lived my life exposed to America's majority culture and, from time to time, I would visit a similar culture in Canada. But those first three days in Korea were my first exposure to an entirely foreign culture. Everything was different. Not subtly different, like the way the Cubics served spaghetti with the sauce on top of the pasta, a difference that blew me away as a child because my family served spaghetti with the sauce already mixed in—

but *completely different.*

But my concern about Korea was put to rest. We all seemed to be treated the same: non-Koreans first, visitors second, and Americans third.

*

Sakaide

As to be expected when having fun, time flew by, and our stay in Korea came to a quick end. We all were thinking that it would only get better as we boarded a plane headed to Osaka. After a short flight, we found ourselves breezing through customs once more.

Osaka was where the Adventure and Horizon groups split up. I told Mark that I would come and see him when I got the chance. He jokingly said that if he ran out of things to do in the city, he would think about coming to visit me out in the country.

My Horizon group jumped on a plane headed for Okayama. Once we arrived, we were met by a staff member of Keihan Fisherman's Wharf named Mr. Hibi, who would be in charge of our general welfare while we were in Japan. Mr. Hibi was what we came to know as a typical salary man. He wore a suit, worked all day and night, drank after work with his co-workers, and never saw his children.

From the airport, we took a bus to our new home. Along the way, we were told about some of the impressive things we saw outside the bus

204

window, such as the Great Seto Bridge. It spanned the width of the Seto and was by far the most impressive thing that we encountered. At the time, it was the world's fourth largest bridge and longest suspension bridge, with four lanes running in each direction on its top deck and two train lines running on its bottom deck.

Mr. Hibi pointed out several islands that supported the bridge and proudly told us about the engineering that was involved in its construction. One was the islands that he pointed out was Yashima, home to about thirty residents and Keihan Fisherman's Wharf, our new workplace.

We arrived at our final destination during the late evening. Right at the sidewalk, we were greeted by about a dozen Keihan staff members, who made sure that we knew that they were there to help in any way possible. Although the staff members spoke very little English, the heartfelt message was loud and clear.

We stood out on the curb, staring at our new home in Japan's countryside, if you could even call it that. It was across the street from a small public park that bordered a six-story hotel. Around the corner from the hotel was a decently sized shopping complex with a huge retail store called Super-Mart.

Our new residence was a compound of sorts. It was located in the middle of a block and flanked with houses. There was a waist-high white gate that surrounded the property, and the apartments were set back about fifteen yards from the gate. Everything looked nice and tidy.

The apartment building consisted of a row of six apartments on the ground floor and six on top of those. It reminded me a little of the motel back in Virginia Beach. Before heading into our apartments, we were given a brief tour of the property.

Behind the apartments was another building, which consisted of classrooms and a large lounge that could seat twenty people comfortably in case of a special event. There was also a kitchen, men's and women's bathrooms, and laundry room. We learned of our room assignments and ran through a checklist of things that Keihan supplied for our apartments.

My apartment was the first one on the second floor on the left side of the building. The door was unlocked, and the keys lay on a small table inside. It was tiny. The kitchen, living room, bathroom, dining area, and bedroom were all in a box about three hundred and fifty square feet. It was one of my first experiences with how Japanese people do things differently. Not wrong or right; just different. Readily visible was the dual kitchen and dining area. The living room had just a small TV with no other furniture.

However, the bathroom was unlike anything I had ever seen. It was sectioned off into several parts. There was a sink with a mirror above and storage space below. The electronic toilet was in its own room, accessible through a door inside the bathroom.

There were sliding frosted glass doors on an adjacent wall. Inside was a room with a tile floor, about four feet wide and six feet long, next to a tub that was about two and a half feet deep, and two feet wide by two feet long. Hanging on the wall above the tiled area was a shower head. The overall layout made it possible for three different people to use the toilet, sink, and bathtub simultaneously. Although I had never seen such a design, I understood the genius of it immediately.

There was an extremely wide closet off the South wall of the living room that was concealed by sliding doors with decorative painting. In it were a bunch of covers, a thin mat with three partitions that folded in on themselves, and an extremely heavy looking comforter. I stood there looking right at a futon wondering where my futon was.

The closet had a shelf about waist high. Just when I had put my suitcase under the shelf and closed the closet, Hugh barged in to ask if I had figured out how to use the tub. I was one of the oldest, but definitely not one of the wisest. I could only shrug and admit to him that I had no clue.

Kyle was next to run into my apartment, asking whether we had figured out how to operate the heating and cooling unit. I hadn't even discovered it yet. He pointed out that it was on the wall near the ceiling to the right of the sliding glass doors that led to the balcony. Then Kyle asked if I had figured out how our electronic toilets worked. "Nope," I said."

As Kyle was showing me how to use a toilet, Kayla came in. The addition of a fourth person in my tiny apartment instantly tipped the scale from crowded to packed. Kayla asked if we had discovered the shutters covering the sliding glass doors of the balcony. Apparently, they appeared suitable for a bomb shelter. I coughed up another "nope."

With our shoes off, we shuffled across my living room to inspect the sliding glass window. I pulled back the vertical blinds, opened the sliding glass doors, and looked down at a two-foot wide balcony. There were indeed bomb shelter-type shutters attached to the outside walls.

Passing by the TV on the way to the window reminded me of something that Mark regularly told me. "Besides having a Japanese girlfriend, watching TV was one of the fastest ways to learn the language." It was suggested that we leave the TV on at all times. So, I eagerly turned the on the TV.

After three months of intensive Japanese studies, I still could not understand a damn word. Neither could anyone else in the room. But, we all more or less figured out that some guy had cars that he was trying to sell at a discount.

We had been there less than an hour, but it felt as if we had been opening Christmas presents all day long. We started to explore the community center and its rooms. The lounge was relatively spacious; we all could sit on the couches without feeling crowded. The kitchen was basically a bigger version of our own kitchens. The classrooms were small, with a portable blackboard and some chairs, and the laundry room had a few washing machines.

I was the first to notice the lack of dryers, and that is when Theo told me about using the balcony as a spot for a clothesline. We quickly realized that Theo was the supervisor to go to if we needed answers, and Pam was the supervisor to go to if we wanted to hear a complaint related to Japan.

Several hours after our arrival, we had settled down enough to go our separate ways and turn in for the night. Standing in front of my door, I couldn't believe that I was standing on the other side of the planet. I had to find the moon. I hoped that it would look different. I thought that there had to be something different about the moon from that angle.

When I found it in the night sky and discovered that it was the same old moon, I told myself that it was different anyway. Then I climbed in the closet, closed doors, and went to sleep in total darkness.

*

"Working 9 to 5 (Kind Of)"

The kenshusei, as we were called, were split into two teams. My team included Theo, Kyle, Hugh, Margo, and Kayla. The other team consisted of Pam, Anastasia, Agustus, Bella, Wendy, and Jax. One team would go to work while the other team would go to school.

The days following our immediate arrival were filled with greetings from neighbors, soon-to-be Japanese coworkers, and Japanese friends of former participants. There was almost always a parade of people just showing up randomly to introduce themselves. When we were not impressing strangers with our rudimentary Japanese greetings, we were all cramming the language to see the fruits of our labor.

On one of those days, my team and I got the urge to take a break from the studying and greeting that was going on at the compound to explore our new neighborhood. It was remarkable: cars driving on the opposite side of the road, the lack of any litter, the general level of cleanliness. However, even more, remarkable than any other aspect of our neighborhood was the discovery of one of mankind's greatest inventions: the beer vending machine.

We found it nestled amongst several other vending machines on the corner of our block, adjacent to the hotel. The other machines not only sold sodas and candy bars, but they also had cold and hot sandwiches, soup, shirts, panties, adult videos, and all manner of treats and trinkets. If you could fit it in a vending machine, it was sold in a vending machine.

The best part about beer vending machines was the fact that it made beer available even if the markets were closed. For those participants under Japan's legal drinking age, no ID was needed. And best of all: the beer was just 120 yen—about a dollar. We all spent a considerable amount of time wondering how this could exist in such an apparently calm and courteous society. Why weren't we fighting in line with groups of underage Japanese kids trying to buy beer illegally?

"Japanese kids do as they are told and do not buy beer from vending machines." Is what our new Japanese friends were telling us during our official welcoming party. We would look blankly at them wondering; "are these people serious?"

At this shin-dig, we were formally introduced to our respective teachers for Japanese language, flower arrangement, cooking, tea ceremony, and calligraphy, as well as the staff that we would work with at the three different restaurants at Keihan Fisherman's Wharf for the next nine months.

This party was the first time I was able to observe Japanese people in their natural habitat. In general, the Japanese people we met on Shikoku were smaller in stature than the Koreans we encountered in Seoul. Compared to Americans, they spoke very quietly. The Japanese people were practically whispering, making the conversations among kenshusei sound like a shouting match by comparison.

As a young man from Detroit, I could not help but notice how safe I felt compared to anywhere else I had ever been. In fact, we had been in Shikoku nearly a week, and I had yet to move the key to my apartment from the kitchen table. We had even gone into Takamatsu, the closest major city on the island, and come back after midnight with all of our doors unlocked and our valuables untouched.

Theo and Pam told us stories of former students leaving wallets and purses full of money on the train, only to have them show up the next day at the police box. It was also normal for the same thing to happen to forgetful Japanese people. Theo himself once left a very expensive camera on the train, and the next day it was at the police box waiting for him.

My upbringing had instilled a constant sense of vigilance and wariness. One just had to assume that there was always a threat lurking somewhere. The safety of Shikoku was a serendipitous culture shock.

*

"Jikan Desu, It's Time"

My team's first day of school was the other team's first day of work. As they went off to their jobs, we stayed behind in our apartments. I was preparing myself to arrive to class on time, but apparently being on time was

211

being late in Japan. Well before our class started, our teacher came and knocked on my door to declare, "Jikan Desu!" She was making sure that I would be able to arrive to class not merely on time, but early. A class that was about 30 yards away.

The gesture seemed anachronistic, yet so quaint as to be almost comforting. I had to glance in the mirror to reassure myself that I was a grown man and not a small child. For a second, I suspected she would go into my closet and pick out my clothes for me as well. Anyway, I took it all in stride. Mrs. Kobuse was an amazing lady in her sixties. She rode a bike from who knows how far away to teach us Japanese.

Even though she was fluent in English, she hardly ever spoke a word of it to us kenshusei. She would struggle with us, trying to convey our messages with nearly non-existent Japanese language skills.

Often, we looked like we were playing charades. As frustrating as it was to learn one of the world's hardest languages, it was both an awesome and purposeful struggle that I was in love with.

When the other group of kenshusei arrived home from work, we got the scoop on things. Everyone said that they mainly just stood around because it was the slow season. They learned how to do some routine tasks, repeated the most important greeting, Irasshaimase, a lot, and met lots of employees that did not attend our welcome party. They also toured the wharf, which they said was beautiful, and found out that it offered tours of the Seto Inland Sea by helicopter and boat. All in all, they had a great time.

212

After we all had debriefed one another about the day, we walked around town, mainly window-shopping and stopping at a beer machine here and there. All around, Japanese people showed us genuine affection and interest. However, Margo and I got a little more attention than the others. This was mainly due to her red, flowing locks and my complexion. But it wasn't animosity, just curiosity.

Contrary to my cousin's warning, Japanese people really seemed to like me. I was the first black person to participate in the Horizon program. Often, I felt pretty sure that I was the first black person to step foot on the island of Shikoku, considering the way people would stop, stare, and smile at me.

On rare occasions, there were even people, from kids to senior citizens, who asked to touch my hair. When I first received the request from a little kid, everyone around found it cute and innocent. However, when an otherwise well-meaning but clearly intoxicated elderly Japanese salary man asked, his curiosity was met with looks of anxious anticipation of my reaction from my fellow kenshusei.

Indeed, his interest was not seen as the same naive gesture as the child's. Although his request to touch my hair could be construed as inappropriate, I could sense no malice in his intentions. I felt the way I had in Virginia Beach, increasingly aware that the guard that I kept up was unnecessary. The victimization associated with my black identity seemed more inappropriate than the man's socially awkward request to touch my hair.

I could barely interpret anything the drunken man was saying, but I did not need a translator to understand. His desire to touch my hair came from a place of genuine affection, curiosity and even admiration concerning my black identity. I consented, which was met with sighs of relief from my fellow Americans and the next round of beers.

The night before my first day of work, Pam deliver what she thought was a friendly reminder that because I would be working around food, I would have to shave all of my facial hair. I was told this back in America but was dreading when the day would come. It may be considered very superficial or vain, but in America, I would never consider shaving my goatee.

I considered it part of my brand as a young black male. However, I took solace in the thought that I would not have an audience in Japan who would appreciate the non-goatee aesthetic one way or another.

I pretended to gasp when Pam told me and heard a few of the other students nearby chuckle. Kyle asked what was wrong. I told him that I would be turning twenty-five years old in a few days and had been proudly wearing my goatee since the age of nineteen. I had no idea how I would look without it. Everyone listening thought I was making a big deal out of nothing. That night, I shaved my facial hair completely off for the first time in my life. I felt naked.

When Kyle saw me the next morning, he did not hesitate to make me feel worse by saying, "I understand why you wanted to keep it."

Mr. Hibi greeted us when we arrived at work, then showed us to our stations. We were split up into pairs and sent to our respective venues. There

214

were a high-end restaurant and two cafes. Kyle, Hugh, Margo, and Kayla were assigned to the cafes, while Theo and I went to the high-end restaurant.

Throughout the day, we rotated among restaurants to meet the staff and the administration. While Theo and I stood at the ready at the entrance of the restaurant waiting to greet tourists, Mr. Hibi's boss, Mr. Tanka, showed up to greet us.

His English was about as good as my Japanese, so Theo did all the talking. But, when he looked at me and started to frown, I didn't need Theo's translation to know that there was something wrong. He asked me a question in Japanese, and my vacant stare and shrug indicated that I could not understand anything that he just said. Then, he tried gesturing and using broken English. "You don't look good." Theo looked just as appalled as I did. Our expression let him know that his words were misunderstood. "No. No," he clarified. "You need beard."

Just when I couldn't believe that I had heard him say that, he tried again, "You need beard!" In typical American fashion, I spoke a bit too loud and a bit too slowly:

"Do . . . you . . . want me . . . to grow . . . a . . . beard?"

He smiled and nodded. I was so excited at the prospect of having my beard back that I asked Theo to translate. Theo diplomatically refused to insult our boss's boss and simply said, "Yes, Andre he wants you to grow your beard."

Apparently, Mr. Tanka said, "We want the cool black guy" and walked off. I knew I was leaving America to come to a foreign land, but I had

215

landed in the Twilight Zone. Theo couldn't understand my excitement, and I could not articulate it to him. But, he seemed happy for my happiness, and that was good enough for me.

When we got home, I was so ecstatic that I shared the news about my beard to everyone. It never dawned on me that there were other men there who may have also wanted to grow their beards. Ironically, it was not a guy, but Pam, who brought up the unfairness of it all. Luckily, my other kenshusei felt that my happiness was more important.

My blackness had been a stigma in America. But here, it was valued. That simple gesture by Mr. Tanaka influenced nearly every major decision I'd make in the next few years of my life. Within a week, I knew I would love it in Sakaide. Not only could I get beer whenever I wanted to, but it was also a good thing to look like myself. Indeed, it was okay to be me. The only thing that made it bittersweet was the fact that it was Japanese society, rather than American society, delivering the message.

*

Life in Shikoku

The city of Sakaide was my new home. I would walk into restaurants and be welcomed like a movie star. Patrons would buy beers for my fellow students and me. We were celebrities. At times, I was the main attraction. In fact, I quickly realized that I was an ambassador for black America and took those encounters in stride.

216

I thought it was important to make a positive impression. I was used to people having pre-packaged ideas of what kind of person I might be. Japan felt like another universe.

I'm sure people had some preconceived notions of who I might be, but they were not so rigid or negative. For the most part, I started on a level playing field every time I met someone new.

I was non-Japanese first, American second, and a guest third. It would have been foolish to get offended every time some old lady wanted to touch my hair. I had to assume she was intrigued because I was the only black person she had ever met. If I scowled, she might assume that all black people are scowling malcontents. In Japan, I was the happiest I'd ever been. I felt positive, and I felt black at the same time. It never seemed as though America wanted me to feel that way.

We were living in a tiny town with not a lot to do besides drink beer and study. So, we often found ourselves taking train rides to Takamatsu. Takamatsu was a true city compared to Sakaide. It was no New York, but even compared to Detroit, it had some hustle and bustle to it.

Right away I noticed the increased density of the population, cars battling through traffic, swarms of people lit by neon lights, and flooded bookstores. More impressive than the number of bookstores was how crowded they all seemed to be; just overflowing with people. The first time I pointed this out to the others, Margo suggested that maybe a lot of famous authors do book signing tours in Takamatsu.

We'd searched, but there were never any famous authors. Only books and readers. I immediately thought that there was no way in hell I would see this in Detroit. In fact, I had never even imagined seeing anything like it anywhere.

Whether it was Takamatsu or Sakaide, we would find ourselves hanging out at the shotengai. Those types of shopping arcades did not exist in Detroit. There were seemingly hundreds of identical shops, markets, and bars on both sides of small streets, all covered with a roof. The many intersections for crossing traffic inside the shotengai made getting lost the norm, but we enjoyed the experience nonetheless.

The kenshusei of the past had found a favorite watering hole called Delta Market in Takamatsu. It was a bar that catered to foreigners and the Japanese people who loved them. We would meet non-Japanese people who were teaching English in Japan or working for their respective governments.

Delta Market played rock and hip-hop music and served Western style food like hot dogs, pizza, and hamburgers, along with Budweiser and Heineken. These things were next to impossible to find outside of Delta Market. However, they also sold my beloved Asahi beer as well. Finding a little Western oasis from time to time was nice.

*

Several local Sakaide residents would show up more often than others. They would become friends for life. There was a group of girls that would take us around and show us the local scene, including nearby towns other than

Takamatsu, temples, shrines, and castles. And, there was Kan. He was of Korean descent. He was extremely wealthy, and he wanted us to know it. He would come by late at night and pile the guys and me into his big Mercedes, and then sneak us off. He would spend the equivalent of several thousands of dollars on our happiness in Takamatsu, always upping the ante if we could get a few of the girls to come along.

Kan wanted us to have a good time, but he also wanted us to know that everything in Japan was not as awesome as it seemed. He presented to us our first negative opinion about Japanese people. He told us that because he was of Korean descent, Japanese people often discriminated against him. Whenever he got drunk enough, the subject would come up, and he would see me as a brother in the fight against discrimination. Neither our Japanese nor his English were at a level that could facilitate a deep discussion on the subject. However, he felt it was his obligation to let us know that for many people residing in Japan, it was not the heaven that we were experiencing.

One day, another very interesting person showed up at my door with an acoustic guitar. It was a guy named Ren. He resided in Tokyo as a research physician at one of the major university hospitals. He was a tall and very handsome Japanese guy who could play Eric Clapton's "You Look Wonderful Tonight." The girls loved him. In fact, we all loved Ren. He was as close to a 1970s cool as a Japanese guy could get. His parents lived within walking distance of the compound, and he had been coming by to practice his English with the kenshusei for years. Ren and I became terrific friends and conversation partners, so much so that he invited me to come and see him if I ever made it up to Tokyo.

*

To Feel Loved - Hip-hop

When Golden Week arrived in May, all of us could hold our own in simple Japanese conversation with the aid of a Japanese dictionary in hand. Golden Week was busy as promised, with people coming from all over Japan to see Keihan Fisherman's Wharf and us. We worked nearly ninety hours that week. One of the most amazing things that I remember about Golden Week was how well everyone worked together. Even the president of Keihan Fisherman's Wharf helped in any way he could, including parking cars. This was an amazing sight to see.

I could not imagine the president of Disneyland ever being caught as a valet. Another amazing thing was the attitude toward service shared by the workers. When I worked at Ram's Horn or Oil Express, management told us that the customer was always right. This was not so in Japan. We were told that the customer is God. Talk about upping the ante.

At the end of Golden Week, we had a huge celebratory dinner for our hard work. To start things off the president of Keihan Fisherman's Wharf stood and made a toast in Japanese. He said we were all his trophies. I was pretty indifferent to what he said, but some of the girls seemed to take offense. He said that he was very proud to have us and even prouder for us to meet, greet, and interact with his customers. I was happy that someone was happy I

220

was there, but the girls took it as if he meant we were all his trophy wives. Maybe there was something to it. However, from my point of view, a person has to aspire to obtain a trophy wife and for most of my life people had been aspiring to get away for people like me.

Just as I did when I went to school in North Carolina, I decided anew that I did not want to go back to Detroit. Hell, I did not want to go back to the US. I had not decided to renounce my citizenship, but I was in no hurry to return.

After Golden Week, we were blessed with the opportunity to visit Osaka, Kyoto, and Kobe, all on the company's dime. We went to several temples and shrines in Kyoto, which was breathtaking. Tourists from all over packed the shrines, and the bookstores were just as crowded as the temples.

Kobe was already showing significant signs of recovery from one of the biggest earthquakes in the country's history just a few months prior. It was incredible that less than six months ago, people were being pulled from rubble where we were now walking. Kobe had a very cosmopolitan vibe. We could not get enough of the Chinese food that we found in Chinatown. It was nothing like the egg foo yung or sweet-and-sour chicken that I was used to back in Detroit.

When we arrived in Osaka, we tried to find the tops of the skyscrapers we were walking in between. We were like country kids going to visit the big city. We instantly noticed the differences between the people of Shikoku and the people of the Kansai region. Physically, they were a bit bigger, especially the younger people. They were not as shy as the people of Shikoku. In fact, the people of Osaka were very outgoing and talkative. People would just come up and try to strike up a conversation.

As a black man, I still stood out and was made to feel special, but it was evident that I was not the first black person ever seen on the streets of Osaka. At best, I may have been the first black person seen that month on the streets of Osaka.

Osaka is an awesome city and would come to be my favorite city in Japan, with Kyoto running a very, very close second. In Osaka, we found a place called American Mura, a retail district show-casing all things American. It was an American version of a typical Chinatown in America. Moreover, some nightclubs only played Hip-Hop and R&B, and there were record stores that only sold *"Black Music."* I honestly felt welcomed in Osaka.

*

After Golden Week, the kenshusei started to divide into two groups: those who loved every minute in Japan and those who were ready to go home. The group who loved Japan included Kyle, Jax, Hugh, Margo, Kayla, and me. Our buddy Kan made sure we kept on loving Japan by continuously taking us out and spending ridiculous amounts of money on us.

Towards the end of the summer, I decided to be adventurous and ride my bicycle to Takamatsu instead of taking the train. I explored a few new places in Takamatsu and then found a park to sit in to study Japanese for a while. After that, I ended up at Delta Market.

It was around eleven PM when I decided that it was time for me to head back home. On my route out of Takamatsu was an underground walkway built to make traffic more manageable and safe at a particular intersection. Bike riders and pedestrians would walk down some stairs and enter what was essentially a sprawling room with a makeshift resting area that had a huge stone upon which people could sit. There was even a little waterfall in the corner. It was unlike anything that I had ever seen, and I thought it made for a brilliant idea.

That particular night as I started my descent underground, I began to hear music coming from inside. It was hip-hop music, and it was blasting! I entered the chamber-like room where I saw about fifteen Japanese teenagers practicing hip-hop dancing. I stopped in my tracks. I was surprised at Hip-Hop's mere existence in Osaka, but the sight of these kids took me well beyond surprised. I was halfway across the globe and in front of me were Japanese kids dancing to music that some Americans called the devil's music and considered total garbage. They loved it! It made me a bit emotional.

When they noticed me, they all stopped. One guy ran over and welcomed me with fairly decent English. I was introduced to the group, and I spent the next few hours hanging out with them. One of the members was a Hip-Hop DJ, and he was very eager to show off his very impressive hip-hop music collection. When he didn't have my complete attention, my attention was on critiquing their dance routine. They were practicing for a local Hip Hop dance competition. My relationship with Hip Hop had gone from rapping being banned in the halls of Bishop Borgess to Japanese kids gearing up for a

Hip Hop dance competition in Takamatsu. My mind was blown. As I rode home, I kept thinking that everything that was bad about being black in America was good on Shikoku.

*

Considered an equal participant

As time went on, I became good friends with Jax, the quiet guy with the look of a punk rocker. We would hang out with Kan more than the others; explore on our own more than the others, and drink more than the others. Several weeks after Golden Week, my feelings about Jax being a great guy were validated.

He disclosed to me that he had some drinks with one of our instructors, Professor Elwyn. Dr. Elwyn had three doctorate degrees in the social sciences and was teaching us about Japanese social structures. During a drinking session, Dr. Elwyn confided in Jax his concerns about my future. He worried about what would happen to me after we all got back to the United States. He hoped that I could get on the right track and become a successful person.

Jax became furious with Dr. Elwyn and stated what he knew to true:

"He's already on the right track and successful. What are you talking about? He doesn't cause any trouble, and everybody loves the guy," Jax declared. Then he enumerated several more facts on my behalf, all of which Dr. Elwyn seemed to be oblivious.

"Andre's Japanese is great; he is doing well academically. He studies hard, plays hard, and doesn't bother people. The only reason you would think that he is on the wrong track is because he is black. Professor, I believe that is stupid and racist."

The drinking session ended with Dr. Elwyn sheepishly trying to explain what he meant as Jax got up and left.

I found out about this incident a few days later as Jax and I shared a few beers after work. I was telling Jax about how easy it was just to be myself in Japan. Jax seemed to get my meaning. He'd witnessed the difference between how people reacted to me in Japan and how people like me were reacted to in America. I told him how everything was so positive in Japan and confided that for the first time in my life, I felt simply like an American.

The victimization associated with my black identity was nonexistent in Shikoku. It is hard to explain, but I would sometimes forget that I was black. I didn't feel like a black student studying abroad I just felt like a student studying abroad.

As I continued to contrast the difference between life in Japan and life in America, I inevitably started to break into a woe-is-me narrative of being black in America: about how I was raised in the projects and how life sucks for the black man.

Jax cut me off and displayed an attitude as if I had deeply offended him.

"Wait. Don't you stand here, of all places, and tell me how hard life is for you because you are black. My brother and I grew up on welfare while my mom worked as a waitress. You ended up living in a better neighborhood than I did and attended better schools. Just because you are black does not give you

225

the right to be a victim your entire life, requiring my sympathy and guilt. You are black, and I am white, and we are both standing in Japan, doing what we want to do and doing it well. I just defended you to Dr. Elwyn the other day who was singing the same song about you just in a different key. Both of you guys are stupid for thinking that way. Andre, you've got it good, man."

Jax was either brave enough or drunk enough to tell me how he really felt. Initially, I didn't know how to react. So, I stood in silence. We both stood in silence.

I broke the silence. "You are right! We are in Japan. Let's leave America back in America." We cracked open another can of Asahi Super Dry, said "Kompai," and continued to drink.

*

Dr. Elwyn, Jax, and I were all at a minimum exposed to America's racist society—not necessarily exposed in the sense of being victimized per se, but we were all aware of its existence. Of course, the degree of exposure varies; with blacks typically having a higher level of exposure than non-blacks.

However, as Americans, regardless of race and the existence of America's racist society, we all must participate in America's free market society.

Unfortunately, those individuals who are equated with America's "white culture" are often seen as the only successful representatives of America's free market society.

Consequently, for Dr. Elwyn, who did not know me as an individual, my blackness was my lone identification as a participant in America's free market society.

My blackness superseded my past, current, and present achievements, character, and social behavior. Therefore, Dr. Elwyn, who could not see me as a representative of white culture, could not see me as successful or "*on the right track.*" In his eyes, and most American's eyes, I needed to become *white* to be successful in America's free market society.

However, Jax knew me on a personal level and saw that although I may not have talked like a *white boy* or rocked out to *white music,* I was doing everything necessary to obtain the skills, values, and ethics that would make me a successful participant in America's free market society.

In Jax's eyes, my identity went from a *black identity* comprised on victimization to the identity of an equal competitor in a free market society. I am forever grateful to Jax because he refused to look at me as a victim and forced me to see myself as the master of my own destiny.

*

A Trip to the Biggest City

Theo and I planned a trip up to Tokyo. He wanted to see some buddies that he knew from his last visit to Japan who were currently teaching English, and I wanted to visit Ren.

We decided to take local trains all the way. It is an extremely long trip, but we were both eager to see all the variations of Japanese people and hear all of the local Japanese dialects. Theo and I would ride up to Tokyo, go to the party district of Roppongi to hang out, and then go our separate ways.

We started our journey in late September. As anticipated, throughout the trip, we saw locals going through their daily routines. We took advantage of the local delicacies and beer that was available on train platforms and just soaked it all in.

When we were about two hours outside of the Kansai area, we encountered an old, drunk man obnoxiously bothering everyone on the train. At that point, I could understand enough Japanese to know that he was very disrespectful to the women on the train. He was telling the older women about his disdain for them and his love for younger women. The women just put their heads down and weathered the storm as it passed through the train car. But suddenly, his eyes landed on Theo, and he decided to sit right across from us. He smiled and politely asked how we were doing. We replied to the old man in kind. He asked if we were both Americans. Then, without waiting for a reply, it was lights, camera, action. He fixated on Theo, and his attitude and tone totally changed.

He began speaking very fast, too fast for me to keep up, but I didn't need to understand the words to understand that the words spoken were not nice. The passengers who had been so indifferent to our existence before were now sitting up uncomfortably in their seats, looking on as if they were witnessing a crime.

Theo could comprehend most of what the old drunkard was saying and started replying to his questions. The more Theo showed that he understood, the faster the old man spoke, and the meaner his tone became.

By Theo's fourth reply, I had no idea what the old man was talking about, until I heard the words Nagasaki and Hiroshima. *Oh! I thought.* He must have been blaming Theo for the ills of WWII. Theo was being tortured. No one was coming to his rescue. Due to the limits of my Japanese vocabulary, I could not even help Theo. The verbal assault lasted for one stop, and the old man disembarked. After he had left, people in our vicinity started apologizing vehemently for his behavior.

During the whole ordeal, the old man never once addressed me. Apparently, he held Theo personally responsible for Hiroshima and Nagasaki and complained that Americans were cowards for not fighting fairly. It was obvious that Theo was bothered by what the man said, and it was obvious that the old man didn't think blacks had anything to do with WWII.

Not knowing how to console Theo, and not wanting to be associated with the atrocities of WWII, I took the opportunity to cloak myself in my black identity and just change the subject.

When we arrived, Tokyo was more than I could have imagined. Osaka was crowded, but Tokyo was utterly packed. The entire city felt like a photo booth with ten people snugly fitting inside it. It was immediately apparent that the citizens of Tokyo discovered long ago that everything needed to be very organized when dealing with twenty-five million people. Even a ride on an escalator had a beautiful sense of order to it. People in a rush would walk single file up or down one side, while everyone else would stand single file on the other side to allow the rushers to pass.

The people in Tokyo were just as polite as the rest of the Japanese people I had met up to that point, but they were noticeably quieter on the trains. It was a bit disconcerting to be on a train packed with more people than oxygen and be able to hear a pin drop. No one was talking. Everyone was looking down, dozing, or reading a newspaper. I felt a weird reluctance to say anything aloud to Theo lest we be culpable for breaking the peace.

Theo and I made our way to Roppongi. We stopped at several beer vending machines and ate pizza at Pizza Hut, which we hadn't eaten since Michigan. I was genuinely surprised by the diversity in Tokyo, which was evidenced by my presence being no big deal *at all*.

With our pizza in hand, we took a seat on the steps of some random building. We had no idea, but we had secured front row seats to what would become a parade of partygoers.

Drunken Australian men were stumbling by, inviting us along for drinks; followed by drunken Irishmen extending the same invitation; in turn followed by drunk American girls who totally dissed Theo. I felt sorry for him. First, the old, drunk Japanese man gave him a hard time, and now his own people were insulting him. I had to laugh at him for that, but he took it well. He did a lot better with the inebriated Australian women who came by next, who joined us on the steps to drink some beers. Theo was in a much better mood when they eventually left. He was drunk and ready to party.

I noticed that there were a lot of African men walking around Roppongi passing out flyers for clubs. I was later told that most of them were Nigerian. They utilized pretty aggressive marketing tactics. I saw some literally snatching Japanese girls into clubs, which would force their boyfriends to follow in a panic, only to receive two free drink cards and a big smile welcoming them to go inside. I found the Nigerians' behavior ridiculous. Worse still, I started to notice that I was not getting the friendly smiles that I had grown accustomed to in Japan. I was being avoided. It dawned on me that I had unwillingly taken on the identity of a Nigerian club hustler.

Around six, Theo and I solidified our plan to split up from Roppongi. In two hours, I would go to Ren's apartment, which was about thirty minutes away, and Theo would go to meet his friends somewhere several train stops away in Shibuya. We needed to kill some time without getting too drunk, so we decided to walk around a bit more. Before we knew it, we were being pulled into some club by a big, intimidating Nigerian man.

"Hey, brother, you want to party? I have a place where there are Japanese girls looking for black guys. Only black guys and Japanese girls."

As I wondered whether the guy had noticed that Theo was clearly not black, Theo replied, "No, you don't." His drinking was catching up to him.

The Nigerian was unfazed. "Come on. Let's go. I guarantee you will want to stay and party."

"Hey, Theo, he guarantees it," I said. Then I asked the Nigerian, "How much to get in?"

"One thousand yen—basically ten bucks—and you get two drink tickets."

"Let's go in!" I said.

Theo and I were led into an elevator that opened to the sound of hip-hop. A Japanese girl sat behind a desk taking money and giving out drink tickets. The club's entrance was covered by thick red curtains from floor to ceiling. As promised, when we went in through the curtains, there were four or five black guys and about fifteen Japanese women.

This was something new to both of us. I had never been in a bar where black men were the main attraction and white men were completely ignored, and neither had Theo. It was awesome.

On the other hand, Theo was obviously not having a good time. Drunk, uncomfortable, and white, he consistently stuck within three inches of me, and he was making me nervous with his increasing state of intoxication. He started to claim he was being discriminated against because the ladies did not want any white guys. I had to chuckle at his inability to handle five minutes of social inequality. I figured it was time for us to go.

We migrated to our previous spot on the steps to watch the ongoing flow of partygoers. Every so often, someone from some part of the world would stop by and talk. There were girls from Brazil, with whom we could only communicate in Japanese. There were French girls who spoke Japanese, but I preferred to hear their English thickened with their French accents. We were both having a ball again.

When it was time to split up, I hopped on the train to Ren's apartment, and Theo hopped on another headed to Shibuya. Tokyo's train system is arguably the eighth wonder of the world, and I was proudly able to navigate it to find Ren's apartment. After an uncharacteristically rushed greeting, Ren said that we had a busy night ahead of us. He had a late dinner with one girl, drinks with another girl, and then clubbing with two other girls all lined up for the evening. We hopped in his new BMW 3 series with the urgency of paramedics leaping into an ambulance.

We met the first young lady at a quaint family style restaurant. She was a sweet looking girl who was working at an office somewhere in Tokyo. To my pleasant surprise, she was very impressed that Ren knew me. She was also thoroughly impressed with his English. I was icing on the cake, and the cake was Ren a handsome, young, single doctor who could also speak English.

The next young lady was more impressive than the first. She was a charming, aspirant, young professional working at a very prestigious company. She spoke English fairly well and was impressed that Ren knew me, but not overly impressed like the first lady we met. That made me feel a bit more like a human being and not some type of puppy or trophy.

Round three for the evening was the best. Ren and I were hanging out with two superstars. One was a surgeon and the other a businesswoman who traveled the world. Once we were introduced, I noticed that it was the first time that I felt as though I had to step up my game.

They saw me for who I was—a college student studying abroad. It felt refreshing and disappointing at the same time. Just being me was great, but not impressive enough to elevate me to rock star status in their eyes. There was no animosity towards me for being an Afro-American, but, unlike the first two girls, they did not find an Afro-American in Japan to be mind-blowing. They could only be impressed by my individual merits. To be honest, it was a bit intimidating. Both women had done what I was doing and currently doing more impressive things.

With smiles on their faces, the young ladies peppered me with what seemed like qualifying questions.

The surgeon asked, "What will you do after you graduate?"

"I'm thinking about law school."

Expressing no astonishment, the businesswoman followed up, "What kind of law are you thinking of practicing?" Totally genuine, she paused for my response.

It occurred to me that she was taking me seriously, and I needed to do more than simply grin back at her. I just blurted out "International Law," though I had no idea at the time of what kind of law I would practice.

The girls drilled me on what I had been studying besides the Japanese language, instead of the common questions I would get from new Japanese acquaintances, such as "can you use chopsticks," "how do you like Japan," or "what's your favorite Japanese food?"

Moreover, they demanded that I speak to them in Japanese. With my trusty dictionary, and some help from Ren every now and then, I did my best to comply with their friendly yet stern request.

As I struggled through the night with broken Japanese over blaring speakers at the various dance clubs, I eventually came to feel that I was a welcomed member of their circle of hardworking young people instead of as a job applicant. We partied and bar hopped until four in the morning, but the fun ended when the surgeon quietly said she had to get some sleep before an early morning surgery. I asked Ren if she was kidding and he replied, "I have no idea."

Ren and I went back to his apartment, where I went to sleep on the couch. I woke up to a note that read, "Went to the hospital. I should be back around 3 PM. Here is the key to the apartment. Have fun, and I'll see you later."

I wandered around Ren's neighborhood for about an hour, only to return to his apartment and watch Japanese TV. The night before had kicked my motivation to learn Japanese into a higher gear. I wanted to take in as much as I could as soon as I could. I figured, hey, you never know, there could be a career as a Japanese surgeon in my future.

My evening with Ren was relatively quiet compared to the night before, and before I knew it, I was headed to the bus station to meet up with Theo and head back home. I asked him if he had a good time and he said it was only okay. He had spent most of the time in his friend's apartment drinking and catching up. Playing down the truth, I told him that Ren and I hit up a few bars and had a pretty good time.

*

After returning from Tokyo, I decided that I definitely had to come back to Japan sometime in the future. I was having too much fun. I was learning so much. I was treated like a prince most of the time. Other times, I was treated like a true rock star with random kids and adults running up for an autograph or photo. Everything about me was good in Japan.

In November, all of us kenshusei started having farewell parties thrown on our own behalves by friends we made throughout the year. I was no exception. My hip-hop friends planned a party at Takamatsu's biggest club and said that I had to come. I invited a Japanese girl named Akiko who would come by the compound from time to time to accompany me to the party, and she agreed.

She had participated in a study abroad program in some remote place in Wisconsin and spoke excellent English. When we arrived at the club, there was a line to get in. A guy at the door taking money saw us, whisked us into the club in front of everyone else, and handed us two drink tickets a piece. He told Akiko that he was told that the black guy was not to pay for admittance, and that applied to my guest as well.

When I walked in, hip-hop was blasting, and the dance floor was packed like a Japanese bookstore. Every time I saw these people dancing to hip-hop and truly trying to embrace its spirit through its clothing and swag, it would nearly bring me to tears. I never intended to represent hip-hop, but I

236

was as close to a Biz Markie, Eric B., and Rakim, or A Tribe Called Quest as they were going to get, and they truly appreciated it.

When the leader of the dance group, a guy named Hiroshi, noticed that I had arrived, he ran on the stage where the DJ was spinning and started speaking in his ear and pointing at me. I waved at them, and then the DJ picked up the needle. The dance floor came to a standstill, and the crowd started to murmur until Hiroshi grabbed the mic, saying "testingu, testingu, testingu."

My friend started pointing at me again, which caused all the eyes that were not already on me to get on me. He began giving what sounded like a speech. Sadly, I could not understand what he was saying. My Japanese was from a textbook, and these guys spoke the local Sanuki dialect with teen slang thrown in. However, I could pick up words such as hip-hop, and sensei, and Andre-san. Akiko interpreted the rest for me in real time as everyone started to give Akiko and me about five feet of space on all sides.

He was telling the crowd how we met, and how I gave them pointers about feeling the music and not just counting steps. He said that we were all brothers and he was so happy that we met. Suddenly, everyone started clapping enthusiastically. Akiko said the applause was all for me. She was thoroughly impressed, and I was awestruck to the point of tears.

I was handed the mic, and in front of a crowd of about five hundred Japanese hip-hop fanatics, the best I could say was simply "Domo arigato gozaimasu." I was too nervous to attempt anything else in Japanese, so I continued on in English and let Akiko interpret. When I finished, there was another round of applause, Hiroshi said Thank you, and then the music started up again.

The five feet of space around Akiko and me immediately shrank back to its previous five centimeters. I was getting high-fives and thank-yous as we walked throughout the crowd towards a table in the back. For a while, we both just sat in amazed silence.

As the last days of our stay approached, we had an official farewell party at Keihan Fisherman's Wharf. We were encouraged to invite all of our friends so that they could celebrate with the Keihan staff who we had worked with for nine months. After the party, the finality of it all was hitting us hard. As for me, I never wanted to leave.

I was treated so nice for simply being myself, a young black man from Detroit. Soon I would have to go home where I was often viewed by others with the same stigma as a felon, suspect, underachiever, or, at best, a second-class citizen.

Although we were headed to Hawaii for a four-day vacation before our return to Michigan, I felt as if I was headed to jail. My worst day in Japan had been better than my best day in America.

Chapter 9

Unwelcome Back to America

Kyle, Hugh, Jax, and I formulated a game plan while in the air headed to Hawaii. We would go to the hotel, check in, and head straight to the University of Hawaii's library to find another program that would send us back to Japan. As the rest of the gang ran towards the beaches of Waikiki, the four of us ran toward a bus that would take us to campus.

After a few hours of searching, we came across Kansai Gaidai University in the city of Hirakata, Osaka. The university had a program that accepted foreign students for a special Japanese studies curriculum that lasted for two semesters. We had found our way back.

Meanwhile, I was back at home with all of the things that went with being black in America. No one ran up to me and asked for my autograph, or asked to touch my hair, or giggled when I walked by. Instead, I would bring a degree of intrigue to an otherwise uneventful security guard's job at numerous retail establishments. In January of 1996, I started classes at EMU and shared an apartment with Mark. He was my best option. No one could relate to what I had just experienced except for someone else who had experienced it. Hugh, Kyle, and Jax got an apartment across the street, and we all joined a Japanese language club to keep our skills fresh.

The friends I had at EMU when I left for Japan wanted to hear all about my adventures. At first, they thought it was cool to hear me speak in Japanese and would happily show me off to others by asking me to say something in my new language. For some, it was like seeing a magic trick.

I knew it was odd to see a black guy speaking Japanese, and even stranger to see a Japanese person and me talking and joking in Japanese. However, my friends started to tire of me talking about Japan, as though it were some kind of heaven on earth that they were not able to reach. I was a Japanese nut. In class, I took notes in Japanese, and I was carrying around a Japanese dictionary everywhere I went.

Toward the end of April, Jax and I both were notified that we were accepted to Kansai Gaidai University and would start classes in the fall. We both received a scholarship from the Japanese government as well. I would come out ahead financially, with a lot of beer money to boot. A few days later, Mark was notified that the Japanese Ministry of Education had awarded him a scholarship to Denki Tsushin University in Tokyo.

Hugh, meanwhile, would be headed back to Japan as a supervisor on the Japan Adventure program. Kyle decided to forgo returning to Japan immediately but would be leaving EMU in the fall to transfer to the University of Michigan. I felt great about my prospects, but what made that period so remarkable is that we were all hitting the jackpot simultaneously and excited about one another's success.

Black and Yen

"Racism is the lowest, most crudely primitive form of collectivism. It is the notion of ascribing moral, social or political significance to a man's genetic lineage—the notion that a man's intellectual and characterological traits are produced and transmitted by his internal body chemistry. Which means, in practice, that a man is to be judged, not by his own character and actions, but by the characters and actions of a collective of ancestors.

Racism claims that the content of a man's mind (not his cognitive apparatus, but its content) is inherited; that a man's convictions, values, and character are determined before he is born, by physical factors beyond his control. This is the caveman's version of the doctrine of innate ideas—or of inherited knowledge—which has been thoroughly refuted by philosophy and science. Racism is a doctrine of, by and for brutes. It is a barnyard or stock-farm version of collectivism, appropriate to a mentality that differentiates between various breeds of animals, but not between animals and men. Like every form of determinism, racism invalidates the specific attribute which distinguishes man from all other living species: his rational faculty. Racism negates two aspects of man's life: reason and choice, or mind and morality, replacing them with chemical predestination."--Ayn Rand, *The Virtue of Selfishness.*

Around the end of spring, I found myself running low on funds between student loan checks, so I decided to dip into the three thousand dollars that I had saved while I was in Japan. I brought the money home via

American Express traveler's checks denominated in Japanese yen. I went to a bank on EMU's campus to cash about two hundred dollars' worth.

I was not an account holder at that particular bank. But, after a brief conversation about my time in Japan and how one could take advantage of the programs that I had discovered, the white girl behind the counter handed me my money.

A week or two later, I went to an off-campus branch of the very same bank. It was located in some city between Detroit and Ypsilanti. I told the white lady behind the counter that I had just returned from Japan and needed to cash a few of my traveler's checks. The lady took my traveler's checks and asked hesitantly if I had an account with the bank. I politely said no, but that I had cashed identical traveler's checks at the EMU branch a week or two ago.

With a heavy sigh, she replied, "We cannot give you twenty thousand dollars, sir."

I smiled and gently explained, "Look a little closer at the checks. They are in yen. Twenty thousand yen is the equivalent of about two hundred U.S. dollars." Her mind was already made up. "I don't know about all of that, but we will not cash these."

"Why not?"

"It is up to my discretion, and because you are not a member of the bank, I'm deciding not to cash the checks." Her curtness in the face of my politeness rubbed me the wrong way. I asked to speak to her manager. She gave me some attitude, got up, and went to get her manager, a tall white man in his forties, who had been looking my way since I walked into the branch.

242

They had a brief conversation and then came over together. He did not have to say a word. I knew he was taking her side.

With a look of indifference, he said, "Hello, sir. I understand that you are not a member of this branch and that you would like to cash twenty thousand dollars in traveler's checks."

With a smirk, I looked at the lady who clearly understood that it was twenty thousand yen and not dollars and politely reiterated, "The traveler's checks are denominated in yen. It is only about two hundred dollars after the currency conversion."

His reply was a dismissive "Because you are not a member, we have decided not to cash these checks. I suggest you go and try to cash them at EMU."

It was yet another negative interaction between myself and some white people in America. The bank teller and her manager assumed that I was trying to commit a crime, which led me to assume that they were two racists.

I looked at both of them and asked, "If I was white would you cash them?"

"No, we still would not cash them."

As I turned to walk out, I yelled, "You will be hearing from my attorney."

I left the bank and started driving toward Detroit. I was going to my grandmother's house to pay a visit and find an attorney in the phone book while I was there. However, by the time I got there, I couldn't shake the thought of how such a thing was so unlikely to happen in Japan. At least I would have been offered the opportunity to become a member of the bank. The anticipation of going to Japan and escaping situations like these granted me more solace than the possibility of a huge monetary reward from a discrimination lawsuit.

Perhaps I would feel vindicated if those two lost their jobs and I got a lot of money, but I did not believe it would change anything in the big picture. Even if I used the money from the lawsuit to open my own successful bank, it was quite possible that the exact same thing would happen to me again at another bank in another city in the future. Returning to Japan just seemed to be a better form of redress.

Some good things happened while I was back in America. I made three good Japanese friends. There was a guy named Daisuke from the city of Kobe who came to America to learn English and play baseball; a girl named Midori, from Tokyo, who was in the States to learn English and date American men; and a girl from Nara, named Fumiko, whose parents were filthy rich and was in the States just to get out of the house.

We would hang out, party, and speak in Japanese as much as my brain could handle. Though the time inevitably came for me to leave my new Japanese friends and old American friends behind in Michigan, I did not hesitate to jump on that direct flight with Jax from Detroit to Osaka.

Chapter 10

Welcome Back to Japan

Jax and I arrived at Kansai Gaidai University in Hirakata, Osaka. The campus was small relative to America's sprawling universities, but it was beautiful nonetheless. The first impression we both had was that everything was extremely clean.

Jax and I settled into our temporary housing in the on-campus dormitory. There were hundreds of exchange students from across the globe participating in the program. Once other students found out we had already lived in Japan for nearly a year, Jax and I were immediately regarded as veterans and experts.

Without skipping a beat, Jax and I found the nearest beer vending machine and started celebrating life. We eventually found some like-minded friends and showed them our unique way of studying Japanese language and culture through a beer can.

The following day, we attended a welcoming celebration for all of the foreign students participating in the program. We were seated in a theater and announced one by one to come up on stage and introduce ourselves. The Americans had the biggest percentage of representatives. However, there were students from Australia, New Zealand, France, England, Russia, Germany, Brazil, Kenya, Nigeria, Canada, Mexico, and Chile.

There were three other black guys from the States as well. Jax and I befriended a black guy named Mack, who was from Chicago with a perfect 1970s-era afro, as well as a guy from Texas named George, who was of Mexican descent.

I was not as special in Osaka as I had been in Sakaide. I would not cause any car accidents from a double take caused by seeing a black person walking down the street. However, I was very much welcomed by the students, staff, and even random people we encountered. The foreign staff was primarily made up of Americans, including a black man named Mr. Davidson. They were there to teach us regular college courses such as politics and business, but with a focus on Japan.

Jax and I both had arranged to live with a host family to help with our Japanese skills and really learn about Japanese culture. Coincidentally, so had George and Mack. I was considered extremely lucky because of my host family. Compared to George's, Mack's, and especially Jax's—the Watanabe family was a jackpot.

Mr. Watanabe was a salary man, who was never home on weekdays. I would only hear him come home at night and leave early in the morning. On the weekends, when I would see him, casual conversation in Japanese and Asahi beer flowed naturally between us.

Mrs. Watanabe was an angel. She made me breakfast and dinner, and always left an ice-cold beer waiting on the table for me. After finishing my homework and eating dinner, we would sit and watch Japanese dramas to

246

improve my Japanese, which was pretty good at that point. However, I still kept a dictionary handy for obscure words.

Mrs. Watanabe insisted that I meet their neighbors, the Kitagawa family. She also asserted that I go out on a date with Mrs. Kitagawa's daughter, Keiko. I met Keiko and thought that she was absolutely beautiful, and knew immediately that I would date her if I had the opportunity. The two women made sure that opportunity arrived, and Keiko and I hit it off quite nicely. That was just another sign of my good luck.

Another reason I was considered lucky was that Mrs. Watanabe would send me off to the clubs after a few beers and tell me to come home in the morning. Jax's host parents would let him go out, but give him an attitude about it and tried to make him feel guilty. George's host parents were really cool, but George thought that they were too young to be host parents, and felt nervous around the wife whenever they were alone in their apartment.

As for Mack's host family, they never really gave him any problems, but he always felt as if he was not what they had imagined for a homestay student. George was turning twenty years old, but Jax, Mack, and I were well into our twenties. Mack had spent time in the Navy and was stationed in Okinawa before arriving at Kansai Gaidai. Whatever image Mack's host family had of a homestay student, I doubt that it was a Navy veteran, with an Afro and black leather jacket who looked like the reincarnation of a Civil Rights Era Black Panther.

Our crew was pretty distinguished on campus, and to my delight, a picture of me studying on the library steps appeared in the school's

247

advertisements for the student exchange program. I would be seen by students across the globe as a positive representation of the students at Kansai Gaidai. Ironically, I did very little studying for my classes. There was so much to learn outside of school.

My Gaidai crew all rode the same train to school, but we boarded at different points, with my stop being the closest. Most days we would walk home, stopping at a few beer vending machines along the way. By the time I got home, I would have another beer with dinner. After dinner, my host mother would ask if I was seeing Keiko that evening, and most evenings my reply was an enthusiastic "yes." Otherwise, I was hanging out with the Gaidai crew. We would go to clubs and bars in the Shinsaibashi and Namba areas of downtown Osaka nearly every Friday and Saturday night. On some nights, we were able to fill a train car with Japanese students from Gaidai to come and party with us. I was living a dream.

When we arrived at the bars and clubs, we were welcomed as long-lost friends. I did not get the superstar treatment like back in Sakaide, but it was better than anything I could hope for in the States unless I were LL Cool J, Michael Jordan, or some other extraordinary Afro-American.

*

Hip-hop, Part Two

My rich Japanese friend from EMU, Fumiko, arranged for her parents to come all the way to Osaka, pick me up, take me out to dinner, and then to

248

meet her brother and his wife at his home in Nara. I felt odd about it, but I had to agree to it. I did not want to be rude, and Fumiko was always so nice to me.

Her rich parents arrived in a custom-made luxury car. My host parents, as if they were my real parents, came out with me and met them in front of the house. Mrs. Watanabe went as far as pushing my head down for a deeper bow when making the customary greetings. It was something to see. Fumiko's parents whisked me off to a private golf course and country club for dinner.

It was by far the most expensive dinner I had ever eaten. My meal alone was the equivalent of four hundred American dollars. I spoke in my limited Japanese, but it was good enough to keep them entertained. After dinner, we went off to meet Fumiko's brother, his wife, and their infant child.

When we arrived at Fumiko's brother's contemporary home that night, the first thing I noticed was a long, black GM Suburban lowered to the ground with chrome rims. Fumiko's brother had a low-rider! And not just a pickup truck like mine: a Suburban low-rider with rims. I tried not to appear too impressed, but I was.

Inside, I was introduced to Fumiko's brother and his wife. Bose speakers were hanging from the living room ceiling with hip-hop playing as background music. I could not believe I was experiencing this.

The brother could barely say hello in English, so I spoke in Japanese the entire night with the help of freely flowing alcohol. Fumiko called while I was at the house, and I assured her that I was being well taken care of. I also told her how surprised I was by her brother's love of hip-hop music. She then asked if I had seen his CD collection, which I had not.

After I had got off the phone with Fumiko, I asked her brother about his CD collection. He took me into another room where the walls were covered from floor to ceiling with CDs. That alone was impressive, but on top of that, they were all rap CDs. He seemed to be prouder of his collection than his son. He has several copies of the same CDs, for some reason, and he ended up giving me fifteen disks: classics like Eric B. and Rakim's *Paid in Full*, Public Enemy's *It Takes a Nation of Millions to Hold Us Back*, Run-DMC's *Rock Box*, and Kool Moe Dee's *Wild Wild West*.

Eventually, her brother drove me back home in his low-rider, blasting hip-hop all the way from Nara to Osaka. It was a wonderful experience. When I told the Gaidai crew the next day, they couldn't believe it. "I told you, Andre is the luckiest guy in the world," Mack quipped with a jealous smirk.

*

Black History Sensei

One Saturday afternoon, I decided to strike out on my own and explore Kyoto. I wound up in front of a joint with a front sign that read "Jazz Cafe." Why not? I thought. When no one paid me any attention after I walked in, I was somewhat disappointed. They were playing jazz, and I was obviously black, so why were they not making a big deal out of it like the kids in Takamatsu? I soon found out when an older gentleman with an air of refinement sat next to me to start a conversation. The guy asked, "Are you

250

from America?" I said, "Yes." Then the gentleman started out asking me questions about my interest in music.

"Of course, I like jazz, hip-hop, R&B, and gospel," I responded."

"Great!" he said. "Do you listen to Miles Davis?"

"Of course."

"Do you know who was in his first band?"

"Uh, no," I said, already starting to feel dumb.

"You don't? Well, do you know Duke Ellington?"

"Yes."

"Do you know all the instruments he played as a kid?"

"Uh...no."

"You don't? What about John Coltrane?"

"Oh, yeah. 'These are a few of my favorite things,'" I recited.

"Do you know who wrote that song?"

"No," I admitted, convinced of my complete and utter ignorance.

"You don't? Are you sure you are an American?" he quipped.

"Not anymore."

The guy was demonstrating knowledge and respect of my culture, and I was too uninformed to even meet him halfway. He had a few harmless laughs at my expense and then strutted off to the bar to get some coffee. A few moments later, another patron came over. Like the first gentlemen, he naturally figured as a bona fide brother in a jazz joint I would be fluent in American jazz history.

He proceeded to give me the same butt-kicking, focusing his questions on Billie Holiday, Nina Simone, and Herbie Hancock. My lack of knowledge on the subject led him to admonish me to study my heritage. As he put it, "It's the only thing that is truly American." I ended up leaving the cafe feeling as though I had let all of black America down.

*

A few weeks later, the Gaidai crew was stopped at a beer machine in downtown Hirakata on the way home from school when a Japanese man made a beeline toward us. He had a big smile and arms spread out, joyously proclaiming "Black is beautiful!" We all gave each other an *is-this-guy-crazy?* look as he began to rattled off all of the beautiful things black Americans contributed to the world. He was a walking, talking ode to Black History Month.

He spoke with a huge, booming voice which drew everyone's attention. Though he could've been mistaken for being a little crazy, he was definitely socially awkward. And, at times his awkwardness was uncomfortable.

He talked about W.E.B. Dubois and Fredrick Douglass. He did not just mention them as figures in Black American history; he told us what they stood for. He mentioned the book *The Souls of Black Folk* and started to discuss it with zeal and clear expertise. He presented these figures and other black Americans as great individual problem solvers; and that the world was better for the solutions that they presented. It was amazing. He somehow managed to disconnect racism from the accomplishments of brilliant Afro-Americans.

He went into the institution of slavery and how some black people in America owned other slaves. He talked about inventions such as the streetlight and penicillin. Then, he gave props to the first black woman to become a millionaire, Madame C.J. Walker. We all stood in disbelief as though Stevie Wonder had just driven by in a Ferrari. As the guy went on, he constantly repeated "Black is beautiful!" like a Baptist preacher saying Amen at the end of each thought.

Listening to his rendition of Afro-American's greatest hits was pretty cool but we eventually had to cut him off because it seemed like he could go on for hours.

As we walked away, I thought about my encounter with the Jazz heads and the Black History month savant. A feeling of shame came over me. I could talk all day and night about victimization and the plight of the black man, but I was nearly speechless when it came to contributing to a conversation about the wonderful contributions that Afro-Americans have made to the world.

*

Racist?

As the semester's end neared, I was worried by one of the program's stipulations. Although I was accepted to Kansai Gaidai for two semesters, some obscure university rule would not allow exchange students to stay with a host family over the winter break. Nor could we stay in the dorms. Most of the students either returned home or went on a vacation to some place such as Thailand.

Ever since I learned back at EMU that I would need to make special arrangements during the break, my friend Midori told me that I could stay with her and her family in Tokyo. Being polite, I declined her offer while we were at EMU, but Midori insisted. She promised that I would have a great time with her and her brother, mother, father, and grandfather. I told her I would hate to be in Tokyo and not be able to go out to Roppongi to party.

She looked me right in the eyes and said that I could come and go as I please, but I still turned down the offer. She persistently presented the offer again soon after I arrived at Gaidai. In fact, both she and her mother insisted upon it in October. Even though I still had not found a place to stay over the break, something made me continue to decline their invitation politely. Finally, in November, Midori's mother asked my host mother to convince me to stay with them over the break. By then, I still had no arrangements for the winter break and was desperate.

Midori and her mother had been so insistent for so long that I thought it would be rude of me not to accept the offer. I told Midori that I would spend five days with her family and then head back to Kansai Gaidai. Despite the rules, the Watanabes were letting me stay on a little while after the semester ended before going on a little vacation. The idea of staying with Midori and her family was turning out to be a good one, because I could see Mark and possibly catch up with Dr. Ren.

Once things settled, I got some good news from Daisuke. He would be home in Kobe on vacation from EMU, and he agreed to accompany me on the trip to Tokyo via local trains from Osaka. It would be a long journey, but not as long as the one Theo and I took to Tokyo from Sakaide.

A few days before heading out to Midori's house, I called and confirmed that I was coming. I let Midori know that Daisuke and I should arrive between five and six PM, and asked if it would be okay if I met up with Mark the same evening. Midori and her mother assured me that it would not be a problem. My spirits were high after being reassured so emphatically, and Daisuke and I headed for Tokyo. The trip did not present quite the excitement that my trip with Theo had, perhaps because I had already done it before, but it was still mostly enjoyable.

Daisuke's constant complaining about how long the trip was taking was the only low point. It was as though he forgot that we had agreed well in advance to ride the local trains for the entire trip. The high point was eating all of the delicious food on the various train platforms.

Daisuke had arranged to stay with Mark in his dorm while I stayed with Midori and her family. On the train, we passed a snow-capped Mt. Fuji, and several hours later we arrived in a very cold Tokyo in the late afternoon. Daisuke and I met up with Midori at the train station closest to her house in Akasaka. She lived very close to the Asahi Breweries Headquarters, as well as a huge, golden piece of artwork that the artist imagined as a golden torch, but to many people looked more like a golden turd lying on its side. Daisuke headed to Mark's dorm after our brief reunion with Midori, and Midori and I

255

headed to her home, a narrow four-story house, with her brother occupying the fourth story.

Midori, her mother, grandfather, and I sat around chatting. I fielded the typical questions that Japanese people found interesting to ask foreigners. Things were going well until I asked her mother what the rules of the house were.

"Do what you want, but you should try to have drinks with granddad," she said.

"No problem!"

"Are you still meeting up with Mark?"

"Yes, we plan to meet up in Roppongi."

"Roppongi?" she asked skeptically.

I innocently said, "Yeah. It's halfway between here and Mark's place."

"Do you have to go to Roppongi?"

"Sure. It's the halfway point."

"Okay, but you should be back here by eleven PM."

I looked at Midori. "I thought that there was no a curfew."

Midori responded, "I thought so, too."

Anyway, I decided I was okay with it. It would be a short night, but that would be fine. Besides, at least I had a roof over my head. I met her dad when he came home from work, and we all sat down to eat dinner. Everything was going fine. Midori's dad asked me the same questions that Midori's mom

256

asked when I arrived, and we seemed to be getting along well until Midori's mom told her dad that I planned to go to Roppongi to meet up with Mark.

"Roppongi?"

Again, I innocently replied, "Yeah. I want to see Mark. You know, he was the one who got me involved with Japan."

"Oh . . . well, Roppongi. There are some problems with people in Roppongi," he said sternly.

"Please don't worry," I assured him. "I've been there before, and I know who and where to avoid. I just want to have a cocktail with my friend Mark."

With doubt in his voice, he said, "Okay."

I left the house at about eight PM, thinking how ironic it was that he worried about this Detroiter's safety in the world's safest big city. I met up with Mark and Daisuke at a random bar. We all caught up on what was going on in our lives, and Daisuke took the occasion to complain about how small Mark's dorm room was. He had never seen anything like it.

There was barely enough space for Daisuke to sleep on Mark's floor. We all laughed about it. We saw Daisuke like a little brother and did just what big brothers do: make their little brother sleep on the floor of the world's tiniest dorm room.

Before I knew it, it was time for me to go. I did not want to be late. I headed back to Midori's house, making good time until I took one train the wrong way. I thought that it might make me late, so I called Midori and told her out of courtesy. She stressed that I needed to get home by eleven PM. That is odd, I thought.

I ended up being about five minutes late, and her mother did not bother to hide her disappointment. She said that granddad had waited for me to drink with him, but ended up just going to bed. I apologized, but could not understand why her mother was chagrined so deeply. Meanwhile, Midori was looking at me with apologetic eyes and suggested that she and I go upstairs to have a drink with her brother, who had just arrived home from work.

He was a super-cool dude with a huge Michael Jordan shoe collection. We had drinks with him and eventually went back down to the main house. Midori and her mom took me to my futon and showed me the restroom and bathtub. I thanked them, jumped in the bath, and then rolled up inside my futon for the night. It had been a very long day, and I was dead tired.

The next morning, Midori woke me and almost immediately asked, "Did you see any roaches or rats last night?"

What a weird question.

"Uh, no," I responded. "You guys have rats and roaches? This place looks like a museum."

"Well, my mother said that lately, they had some rat issues. You sure you did not see any?"

"No rats," I said. Then I wondered why they would invite anyone to stay with them—on the floor in a futon no less—if they knew big ass rats were running around the house. I figured she meant to say mice.

I got ready and headed downstairs for breakfast with Midori, her mom, and granddad. Her father had already taken off. There was the traditional Japanese breakfast of fish, miso soup, and, to my surprise and horror, mochi. I had been introduced once previously to the white rice pulverized into a gummy paste. I explained in no uncertain terms to Midori's mother the evening before that I could not stand mochi.

Things were getting weird. Of all of the things I knew about Japanese people, being absent-minded about the preferences of a guest in one's home was unheard of. However, the mom was utterly nonchalant, so I pretended as if I had never mentioned mochi the previous evening, and I ate it all with a smile.

Then, as if on cue, Midori's mother brought up the rat issue. I assured her that I had not seen any vermin, and asked Midori what the day's agenda was. She informed me that her relatives from Hokkaido were coming into town and would stay at the house. Apologetically, Midori's mother said that I would have to share a room with an uncle. I found it preposterous that they would fail to mention it until after I arrived in Tokyo, but beggars can't be choosers. So I agreed amicably. Then Midori chimed in with something in Japanese in an unfriendly tone that I could not fully understand, and her mom's expression became desperate.

"Do you plan on seeing your doctor friend while you are here, Andre-san?" her mother asked.

"Sure, at some point, but I have not even contacted him. He is always so busy."

259

Japanese people are known around the world for their sometimes-crippling inability to be direct, but Midori's mother got over that handicap quickly.

"I think you should stay with him."

I could no longer ignore the writing on the wall. I looked at Midori and said, "Midori, you've got to be kidding. What happened?"

Midori looked away as though she had just sold me out to the feds. Midori's mother was apologetic, but this was inexcusable. She had begged me to come and stay in her house. I had not met a Japanese person who had been anything but kind, gracious, giving, and welcoming, but now my friend's mother was kicking me out of her house and into the winter cold of Tokyo. Despite my indignation, I was no longer comfortable being there if I was not welcome.

I already knew that Mark had no extra space at his place, so I called Dr. Ren's cell phone, and he answered. It turned out that he was at the airport headed to Shikoku, and his flight was boarding as we spoke. There was only one option left. I called Mark.

"Yo, this is Dre."

"What's up?"

"Hey, man, I'm at Midori's house, and her mother is kicking me out."

"What?"

"I don't even know what's happening. I woke up this morning, and they basically told me to get the hell out."

Mark started laughing and said, "Hold on a second." He told Daisuke, and I could hear Daisuke laughing his ass off in the background. At the moment, I found it hard to see the humor.

"Mark, I'm serious. It's winter, and these people are putting me out on the street. I need to stay with you and Daisuke for the next four days."

"Four days? Homes, I don't know if the three of us can fit in here."

"Look, if there is any way possible, you need to rescue a brother. It's winter out here."

"All right, I'm not going to let you be homeless in Tokyo. You can try to sleep on top of Daisuke or something. Just hop on the train and come over."

I hung up the phone and turned to Midori and her mother. "I am leaving."

"Midori's mother looked relieved and asked, "So, you will be staying with Mark?"

"No, I can't stay with Mark."

"Well, then where will you stay?" Aki asked.

"Outside," I replied curtly. There was no longer any need for niceties. I retrieved my belongings from upstairs, offered a terse goodbye, and then left the house."

Midori and her family had just taken a big shit on my Japanese streets paved with gold. The night before, all of my interactions with the family members, including the father, seemed as pleasant as any other encounter with Japanese people. We had drinks. We laughed and joked. And then all of a sudden, the joke was on me. I walked to the train station in a daze. I was not ready to relinquish my new world.

Sadly, my first consideration was that her father might not have known I was black. In America, racism would be the reason I was being kicked out. But, up to that point, Japan had been the opposite of a racist society. Japan was the first place where I felt socially equal to my fellow Americans. In fact, if there was a preference for a category of American, it seemed to be for the rare black guy over the more common white guy.

I arrived at Mark's University pissed off and still in a state of shock. Despite my obvious emotional distress, Daisuke could not help himself and teased me mercilessly. Mark spared me with a commiserating grin. After he had been finished clowning on me, Daisuke was the first to suggest that Midori and her mom did not tell her dad that I was a man.

Her dad likely assumed that we had something going on besides being just friends, and he was not having any of that under his roof. However, we were just friends, and Midori and her mom knew that to be the truth. For the next several minutes, we all said very unflattering things about Midori, her mom, and their cavalier approach toward her dad's attitude about his daughter's male friend staying in his house.

Out of the three of us, it was Daisuke, the Japanese guy, who was the first to bring up racism. "Maybe he just doesn't like black people," he suggested. Daisuke instantly reminded me of my cousin Kevin, who would've made that conclusion immediately.

262

It surprised me that racism was not the singular voice drowning out all other possibilities for a negative interaction with someone outside of my race. While I was being kicked out, I just kept going over in my head what I could have said to offend them. *Had coming home a few minutes late warranted their extreme reaction? Was being associated with Roppongi's nightlife that bad? Had they reacted to me personally or to a bad experience in the past that I had unwittingly reminded them of?*

It never crossed my mind to accuse Midori or her family of being racist. I guess I respected them too much as individuals to levy such an accusation without more direct evidence. I needed to hear someone say they disliked black people, but I never did, so I was left to attempt to surmise what the problem was.

Frankly, I wanted to believe that Midori's father decided to throw me out on the streets because she neglected to tell him that I was a man. Though I did not excuse his rudeness, I could at least acknowledge how her father could have been taken aback. I could even understand why he might have disapproved of me hanging out in Roppongi, considering some of the outlandish behavior I had witnessed there.

On the other hand, I could believe that race was more important than my individuality. There was a chance that just being black was a sin that had to be exorcized out of that man's home.

If my crime was merely being black, it meant that her father made his decision out of nothing more than racist spite. However, in believing that this assumption was true, I would also be choosing to see myself as a victim of a permanent stigma based on my race.

Nevertheless, I still had to consider the possibility that Midori's father was racist. If so, it was crucial that I ascribe his beliefs and actions to him alone, and not to his family or Japanese people in general.

I had to see him as a pitiful individual who was neither confident in his daughter's judgment nor decent enough to evaluate me as an individual.

It is not necessarily evil to want to avoid the challenge of getting to know someone of a different race, culture, and language. It is not easy, and there are many opportunities for misunderstanding and bruised feelings. However, it is at best lazy and cowardly, and at worst malevolent, to cause pain and discomfort to a person due to preconceived notions based solely on their race.

As the three of us discussed why this had happened, it was the Americanized Daisuke who kept insisting that the guy was a racist. Meanwhile, I was receiving a deluge of calls from both Midori's cell phone and home phone, but I refused to answer. Midori and her mother both left messages. In several Midori was crying, apologizing, and saying it was her dad who decided that I had to go but would not say why.

After blowing off some steam with Mark and Daisuke, I was back on track. I decided to chalk it up as one strikeout after batting a thousand in Japan. My attention turned to my stomach. I had not planned on supplying food for myself, so I did not have money to eat three square meals a day for four more days. Thank goodness for the local Yoshinoya restaurant. Though

Yoshinoya is ubiquitous throughout Japan and ridiculously cheap, I had never eaten at one.

The first thing I noticed when we walked in was that the menu consisted of a single entree called gyudon. It was a bowl of rice topped off with simmered beef and onions. Other customers who walked in rarely bothered reading the menu because the main ordering option was the size of the bowl rather than its contents.

A humble bowl of soup or a light salad could be added, and I was amazed that customers usually got served within ninety seconds of sitting down. A meal at Yoshinoya was not about dining; it was about ordering, eating, and leaving. We ended up eating at Yoshinoya every day for most of our meals: three dollars for delicious food.

I did not want to upset my homestay parents while they were on vacation in Shikoku, so I did not call them and tell them that I had been kicked out. However, I received a call from my homestay mother the next day, as Midori's mom had apparently called her inquiring about whether I decided to stay with Mark or go back to Osaka. Of course, my homestay mother had no idea of what was going on.

After cursing Midori's mom for kicking me out, she called me. I told her that I was okay and that both Daisuke and I were staying with Mark. I also let Keiko and her mother know about what happened. They wanted to come up to Tokyo and make some heads roll. Despite the chicanery of Midori and her family, I ignored their daily phone calls, and the three of us guys had an awesome time in Tokyo.

265

Daisuke and I headed back to Osaka where Keiko and the Watanabes welcomed me as if I were a returning veteran. When I told the Gaidai crew what had transpired, they all just laughed.

"Ha!" Mack said.

"I guess we can't call you lucky anymore. Oh, wait, you just happen to have one of your best friends living in Tokyo at the time."

*

Guess Who's Coming to Dinner

The next semester, the Gaidai crew and I all relocated to live in the dorms due to stipulations of the school. I was still dating Keiko, so I still saw the Watanabes all the time, and by that time I already knew that I wanted to come back to Japan after I graduated. In fact, I was going to graduate from EMU while I was at Kansai Gaidai. I had heard about teaching English for the Japanese government on the Japanese Exchange Teacher, or JET, program. It would be the basis of my third trip to Japan.

The program paid well, provided health insurance, and disbursed a one-time pension payment upon departure. Though I could request three locations, I could not choose where I would ultimately teach. The one-year contract could be renewed twice, for a total of three years. I applied to the program and requested the cities of Osaka, Fukuoka, and Kyoto.

Prior to graduating, I was informed that I had been accepted to the program and would be stationed in Fukuoka City. However, when I applied for the JET program, it was around early November. Keiko and I had just started dating. By the time I was accepted, we were pretty serious. Though we were happy that I would be in Japan, Osaka and Fukuoka were too far apart for comfort. So, Keiko and I made the decision to move in together in Fukuoka.

Although her mother loved me to death and her brother was very fond of me as well, her father did not know I existed. The word on the street was that he was a very mean, and successful man who worked for Panasonic as a VP of international sales. Due to the decision, Keiko and I had come to; I would have to meet him.

So, her mother arranged for me to come to the house to meet Keiko's dad and tell him that I was taking his only begotten daughter away to shack up in Fukuoka.

I was extremely anxious about announcing such a major event upon my very first introduction. I ran through all of the possible scenarios in my mind, and most of them ended with her dad having a conniption. Agonizing over it was not helping, so I decided my only course of action was to be extremely respectful, put on my best smile, and hope for a miracle.

For backup, I had Keiko's brother, who was a reformed wild child now living on his own and trying to become a responsible adult after a rambunctious youth. I had a great reference from the Watanabes, and Keiko's mom had my back so that that fateful evening would start out three against one.

The big day came, and I had never been so nervous in my life. In my mind, I had already mapped out the quickest route to the exit just in case he pulled out a samurai sword. I showed up in a suit with a bottle of fine sake.

I brought to bear at that moment everything I had learned about Japanese culture and language. I could not afford any missteps. I bowed deeply. My greeting was polite and impeccable. Contrary to my expectations, he was very gracious. Then, out of nowhere, he switched over to English.

It never occurred to me that he would be able to speak English, let alone so well. It turned out to be a surprise to everyone because his family had never heard him speak in English and was unaware of his great handle on the language.

Keiko's mother looked on in astonishment as she heard the man she had been married to for decades conversing in a foreign language. Keiko's brother's English was unfortunately non-existent, so after his initial shock, his interest faded fast.

Then, the conversation turned to the subject at hand. Her dad erased his welcoming smile. In perfect English and with a stern face, he stated, "You know I have a prejudice against your people." My Japanese was much better than Keiko's and her mother's English, but they understood it as if the heavy phrase was spoken in Japanese. Meanwhile, her brother sat there, totally clueless.

The problem with his statement was that it was not obvious to me who he meant by "your people." I did not know whether he was talking about black people or Americans in general. Meanwhile, the women immediately bombarded him with a verbal attack that woke Keiko's brother up from his slumber. As the women continued their assault, I thought that I would not be there long enough to enjoy the fragrant scent of our dinner coming from the kitchen.

While Keiko's brother and I sat there looking as if we were watching a sporting event, I wondered if her dad was a racist or just someone who had childhood memories of geopolitical conflict with America. I could not bring myself to ask. Instead, I decided to make a choice.

One option was to assume the worst about him: that he was a racist who was stupid enough to believe that I was inferior to him because of my ethnicity. Another option was to assume that he saw me as a representative of the country that firebombed Tokyo to smithereens, dropped indiscriminate atomic bombs on Nagasaki and Hiroshima, and forced his country to surrender in WWII.

The old man on the train with Theo and I flashed before my eyes. That guy, who was old enough to have borne arms during WWII, seemed to look at me as if black people had nothing to do with the war. Though I was too afraid to ask, I felt that it was okay to assume Keiko's dad knew that some black people fought in WWII. The reality was that I did not want to know if he was a racist. That would have brought him down a few notches in my eyes.

Up until that point, I had been thoroughly impressed with what I knew of his educational and professional accomplishments, personality, and commitment to family. Moreover, if he were a racist, I would be tearing Keiko apart from her family since I was not going to let her go over anyone's racist

269

beliefs. I felt no deference to racism, and would not elevate it to something strong enough to get in the way of something or someone I wanted.

I chose to give him the benefit of the doubt. I figured instead that he was someone who had a prejudice against Americans—black, white, or otherwise—and that no American had ever had the chance to address and overcome his prejudices. I would take the opportunity to represent all of America in the best way I could.

I could not follow what the women were saying, so it was hard to judge a good time to jump in. Even though my vocabulary was limited, I knew he would take my words more to heart if I addressed him in his language. I bit the bullet and bluntly interrupted with a short monologue in Japanese.

With the utmost sincerity, I stated, "I can understand if you have a prejudice against my people. But, you have no reason to be prejudiced against me. I have done neither you, your family, or your country any harm. I adore your daughter and your family, and thoroughly respect, admire, and appreciate Japan and Japanese culture. Please judge me as an individual.

I am a student at a prestigious Japanese university, on a scholarship from your government, and I plan to go on to teach English for three years in Fukuoka before heading to law school to become an attorney."

I knew he understood every word I said. After a slight hesitation, he opened his mouth to speak. Before he could get a word out, the women jumped back in and resumed their chastisement of him. His utterly calm demeanor was more frightening than the women's vicious tone and body language, so much so that I started to worry that being ganged up on was only making him feel more entrenched in his stance.

However, he was a man full of surprises. Ignoring the verbal battery being thrown his way, he leaned in a little towards me with a relaxed face and said, "Attorney? You don't say. I always wanted to be an attorney, but when I was in college, I became gravely ill to the point that my grades suffered and I had to give that dream up."

With that simple acknowledgment of common interests, calmer heads prevailed, and the discussion lightened up a bit. After a great dinner, some fine sake, and getting to know each other better, I was accepted as a true contender for son-in-law. I got the okay to take Keiko to Fukuoka. We ended the night on a high note. When I returned to the dorm to report back to the Gaidai crew, it seemed like everyone there knew what was going on in my personal life, so I had an audience in waiting. At the end of my retelling of the evening's events, Mack gave me the now customary, "You are just lucky, man."

At the end of the second semester, the Gaidai crew split up to go our separate ways. I headed back home to Detroit for about six weeks before I started my new job in Fukuoka as a sensei.

*

Fukuoka and the Burakumin

I would enjoy three years teaching English in Fukuoka and then return to the States for law school. Just before my trip back to the United States, one of my Japanese English teachers named Mr. Mitsu Inoue asked me

271

if I would not mind speaking before a group of people called the Burakumin, a historically scorned group of Japanese people. He explained that Buddhism required the shunning of these people because their ancestors buried the dead or tanned hides. So, for about four hundred years or so, they had been ostracized by Japanese society. Not giving it a second thought, I politely agreed.

As that day approached, I became more and more disheartened about speaking about overcoming discrimination. Soon, I would be back in America, where the fight against racism was still alive and kicking. Nevertheless, it occurred to me that black people in America had overcome quite a bit, and I could proudly speak about the strides that they made.

When the day came, I was excited about meeting these people. The event was held after working hours in a middle school auditorium. Before my speech began, there was a brief meet-and-greet, and I made my way through the crowd of about fifty to sixty people with my Japanese English teacher Mitsu in tow, introducing me to everyone. During the meet-and-greet, I kept wondering when the Burakumin was going to show up.

If I had learned anything while living in Japan, it was that things always start on time. So when the time came, Mitsu invited me to walk back behind the stage with him. He wanted to say a few words, introduce me, and then have me come out from behind the curtains.

Slightly confused, I asked, "Shouldn't we wait for the Burakumin?"

"They're here. Who do you think you've been talking to?"

I was speechless.

272

Then, I remarked, "But these people look, sound, and act like any other Japanese people."

Looking at me as if I was crazy, he said, "I know," and then headed to the podium.

I was amazed. Discrimination based on physical attributes was so ingrained in my mind that I thought that the Burakumin, who were Japanese, were supposed to look physically different.

Mitsu introduced me as Andre Sensei. The next thing you know, I was telling my tale of woe about racism in my home country. I ended my brief monologue to open the floor to questions and answers by saying that although black America has made strides in the fight against racism, we have a long way to go until it is eradicated. But as I looked into the crowd of people, I had an epiphany.

Until aliens come down from outer space and give us a common adversary to band together against, human beings will always invent some justification to discriminate against our own kind. If these people, who look just like any other Japanese person, were victims of discrimination, a black man in America didn't stand a chance of permanently avoiding it in the States. Eradicating racism is a fallacy. Therefore, the question is not when will we eradicate racism, but how to live the best life possible despite its existence.

After the gathering was over, Mitsu, a few of the Burakumin, and I went out for some beers and karaoke. In every way, they were Japanese. All the way down to the question of "Can you use chopsticks?"

What stuck with me was, they were financially prosperous like my Korean friend Kan. But, more importantly, they seemed to be happy people. Although being a victim of discrimination was a part of their existence, here, it did not define who they were or their potential in the world.

*

Back in it

After nearly six years of being disconnected from America's unjust level of social equality, I prepared for my return. Within minutes of disembarking from the airplane, I could feel the unjust level of social inequity. It was everywhere and inescapable like humidity on a hot summer's day in Detroit.

Despite this reality, I was happy to catch up with family and friends before taking those first steps on that rigorous road to a Jurist Doctorate. Everyone I talked to seemed to be doing well. It is especially great catching up with friends that I had not seen since the days of the red truck. One of my friends jokingly accused me of lying about my whereabouts all these years stating "Come on Dre, just tell the truth—you were in jail."

It was during this brief time in Detroit that I learned that Lea had been murdered. Lea, like so many victims of violence, was in the wrong place at the wrong time. I was told that on the way to dinner, her date realized that he had forgotten something at his house. He turned the car around, returned home and hurried inside. Waiting for him were assailants with guns.

Lea was shot and killed while she sat waiting for him. She and her companion were gunned down by men born and raised in America's racist society. They saw the value of her and her companion as less than zero. The permanence of their race kept their social value at a negative level even amongst their peers.

However, in a free market society, Lea had obtained the skills, and from all accounts adhered to the values and social behaviors that led to success in a free market society. Unbeknownst to Lea, the guy she had just started dating was involved in the drug game. She was killed over a drug dispute.

Some may argue that for her to be successful and alive, Lea should have done what my mother did and disassociated herself from *those crazy black people*. But as I stated in my law school class, blacks should not have to denounce other black people to feel successful. More importantly, no one— black, white, or otherwise—should feel as if they have to move away from black Americans to feel and be safe.

There must be a change in the level of social equality for blacks in America. A change that is initiated *by blacks in America*.

'The first step must be a change in what constitutes the modern day black identity. Unlike the permanence of race, the black identity is not fixed. It can change. It is fluid, malleable.

An adjustment in the right direction will result in affluent predominately Afro-American neighborhoods becoming the norm and not the exception.

Chapter 11

Coming to a Close

"It was in this dull flat, and unthrifty district or neighborhood, bordered by the Choptank river, among the laziest and muddiest of streams surrounded by a white population of the lowest order, indolent and drunken to a proverb, and among slaves who, in point of ignorance and indolence, were fully in accord with their surroundings, that I without any fault of my own, was born, and spent the first years of my childhood."

--Frederick Douglas, Life and Times of Frederick Douglass.

You can go all the way back to Pre-Civil War America to find that this country has operated with two conflicting societies that included several distinct cultures. The Northern States' free market society, in which skills, values, and social behaviors were a person's most important attributes.

The majority of the participants within that society consisted of members of the Puritan and Quakers cultures. Although we typically only think about the religious beliefs held by Puritans and Quakers, their contributions to their society also included a very strong individual work ethic, a zeal for education, high social standards, thrift, and a belief in free labor.

It is important to note that very few black people were exposed to these cultures simply because the overwhelming majority of blacks (around 90 percent) resided in the Southern states.

276

America's South has historically represented America's other society; a racist society in which race superseded skills, values, and social behaviors not only socially but legally. This society was primarily made up of Cavilers from Southern England and the Redneck-Celtic cultures of pre-modern Scotland, Northern England, and Ireland. *(Redneck in this context is not used as an insult but as an identifier of people belonging to a culture that pre-dates America)* Attributes of these cultures included a disdain for labor, violence, sexual promiscuity, self-pride and an aversion towards education

According to David Hackett Fischer's book, *Albion's Son,* and his other works on the subject of cultures that migrated to the New World, things like Afro-American speech patterns, the eating of what American's call "soul food" (like chitterlings), the oratorical style of preaching, the old wedding traditions of jumping the broom, and many other cultural markers widely considered unique traits of Afro-American culture *actually originated in Scotland and Ireland.*

In other words, ghetto super star, your cultural brother resides in the Appalachian Mountains, not the plains of Africa.

Recognition of these distinct cultures is essential due to the very impactful influence the Caviler and Redneck-Celtic cultures had on the vast majority of black people in America.

The importation of slaves from Africa was outlawed over fifty years before America's Civil War. America's slave owners had a preference to breed slaves as opposed to importing new slaves. It is easy to infer that the cultures surrounding the blacks, free or slave, had a major influence on them with distinct African cultures having less and less of an influence over time.

However, African-American culture is all too often spoken of as having a direct and unbroken link to African culture, as if those African cultural traits were continuously being reinforced via osmosis over decades of time and miles of ocean.

Dismissing the essential need for skills, values, and social behaviors needed to succeed in a free market society due to a false representation of black culture has been detrimental to many African American individuals and communities.

*

The Civil War brought an end to the legality of the South's racist society. Subsequent Jim Crow laws succeeded in many respects in reestablishing the legality of the region's racist society.

The 1960s era Civil Rights legislation granted equal rights to blacks putting an end to the legality of America's racist society. However, the equal rights granted to blacks during the Civil Rights Movement did not and *could not* grant a just level of social equality to blacks. Unlike objective legal rights, which can be granted or restored, a just level of social equality must be established. It is established over time by individuals obtaining skills, along with adhesion to positive social values and behaviors.

Booker T. Washington, Frederick Douglass, and P.B.S. Pinchback, the first African American to become governor of a U.S. state, were Civil Rights activists who understood that you can't legislate social equality.

Organizations like the Union League and the Freedman's Bureau established during America's Reconstruction, not only understood this, they supported efforts for the newly emancipated to obtain the skills, values and social behaviors needed to participate in a free market society successfully.

"...The progress, for most blacks, can be measured from the time of the Emancipation Proclamation of 1863. That progress was slow but steady. By 1900, a majority of blacks Americans were literate— something that would not be true of the population of Romania until decades later, and the population of India until more than half a century after that."

--Thomas Sowell, *Wealth, Poverty, and Politics*

After the Civil War, many organizations like the Union League, and the Freedman's Bureau attempted to replace the South's racist society with the North's free market society.

They did this in part by sending representatives of the North's free market society to the South to help educate the newly emancipated, poor landless whites, and Yeomen for participation in the free market society with free labor has its economic underpinning. For a while, the Northerners' efforts produced some remarkable results. Black grandparents and grandchildren alike flocked to the South's newly established public-school systems.

However, the message concerning self-determination by obtaining skills, and adherence to positive values and social behavior despite racist and racism so passionately articulated by Civil Rights activists of the Reconstruction era, has been at best forgotten or at least willfully ignored by modern day-post 1960s civil rights activists. The results are historically low education levels, high crime, and poverty rates for many inner-city blacks.

A just level of social equality can't exist in a racist society. By definition it is unfair. In a racist society, you are born either privileged to belong to the majority or born stigmatized as a member of the minority.

To ever be considered equal in America's racist society, a minority needs a qualifier. Throughout the history of America's racist society, exceptional black individuals have become profoundly rich and famous. From Madame CJ Walker, Oprah Winfrey, Paul Robeson, O.J. Simpson to Shawn "Jay Z" Carter, these exceptional black people can be seen as having obtained that Plessy qualification. They've eliminated most, if not all, of that negative-fifty-million-dollar deficit, resulting in an equal status with ordinary white citizens in a racist society.

A racist society will not allow an unexceptional African American this qualification. However, a free market society in which values, skills, and social behavior take precedence affords ordinary African Americans and everyone else the chance at a successful existence in America.

You can be a successful yet economically poor student, or a successful middle manager, or a successful mentor to children in a free market society.

Simply consider the great amount of educational and economic success seen in modern day African and black Caribbean immigrants. They may experience racism, but like the Burakumin I encountered in Japan, African and black Caribbean immigrants here in America don't seem to be defined by racism.

*

Faith

Have you ever wondered why some athletes could sign a 5-million-dollar contract and feel content riding off in a Ford F-150 pickup truck and other athletes who sign a 5-million-dollar contract spend all of their earnings on exotic cars and mansions?

Or, why having access to the latest gym shoes is more important to a child's parents than having access to great math tutors? Some people have more faith in the influence of a racist society over their lives than the influence that a free market society can have over their lives.

Black people raised in the cult of racism can only see America as a racist society. This outlook leads to an unhappy existence in America. As a black minority in a racist society, whatever you accomplish would be an even better accomplishment if you accomplished it as a member of the white majority. *i.e. you were promoted, but you would have been promoted faster if you were white; you just got a raise, but it would have been a bigger raise if you were white.*

This outlook always provides a racist or systematic racism to impede success and excuses away failures. This perspective sees success as primarily as obtaining the Plessy exception or overcoming the omnipresent racist. A person with this outlook fails to see the hurdles all human beings must overcome to achieve any goal i.e. acquiring a marketable skill-set, overcoming discouragement, ignoring all the people who just don't like you, staying determined even when you're so tired you think you cannot go on, studying hard, etc.

Furthermore, white people who view America as a racist society have ignored, to their own detriment, the need for marketable skills, values, and social behaviors that led to success in a free market society. Simply consider the landless-whites and Yeomen of the antebellum south who had to compete against slave labor to scratch out a living.

Just being white is not a skill-set. You can't just stand in line for your six-figure salary at Google as a software developer. You have to compete for it; and not just against minorities in this country but with people across the globe.

*

In conclusion

Just as you can be too pious to be any *earthly good*, you can also be too focused on racism to be of any value in a free market society.

Far too many black people believe in racism with as much faith and vigor as they do in Jesus Christ. The cult-like belief in racism destroys more black lives and futures than any KKK member has ever dreamed of destroying them. As long as racists exist, racism will persist.

But, you are stronger than racism! Beware of race-baiting social activists, politicians, and TV pundits. Their message is financially beneficial to themselves but socially and economically detrimental to their entire audience, black and white. We all have to ignore racism to the degree we *safely* can, and go out and get marketable skills that others are willing to pay for by all means necessary.

*

Warning

An increase in automation and artificial intelligence are the next logical steps for a free market society. Eventually, people who are living in America's racist society will find their complaints of systematic racism or illegal immigration irrelevant when automation and artificial intelligence eliminate the jobs they are trying to secure. More and more black and white Americans will not only continue to be under employed, unemployed and miserable but quite possibly useless burdens. Unfortunately, the new joke will be: "What do you call a blue-collar worker in Virginia?"

"Unemployed and worthless.